Smart Rescued Animals

81 amazing true stories

'At the Greek Animal Welfare Fund we believe that all animals deserve our compassion and respect. We are delighted that SMARTER than JACK has created a book to show how special and smart rescued animals are – as are their human rescuers.'

Steve Maxworthy, Operations Director (UK), Greek Animal Welfare Fund

Helping animals & connecting animal lovers worldwide

The publisher
Smarter than Jack Limited (a subsidiary of Avocado Press Limited)
Australia: PO Box 170, Ferntree Gully, Victoria, 3156
Canada: PO Box 819, Tottenham, Ontario, L0G 1W0
New Zealand: PO Box 27003, Wellington
www.smarterthanjack.com

The creators
SMARTER than JACK series concept and creation: Jenny Campbell
Compilation and internal layout: Lisa Richardson
Cover design: DNA Design, Lisa Richardson and Catherine Read
Cover photograph: 'Portrait of a Tabby Cat' from Digital Vision, provided by SpecTec Images
Illustrations: Amanda Dickson
Story selection: Jenny Campbell, Lisa Richardson, Anthea Kirk and Hannah Robson
Proofreading: Vicki Andrews (Animal Welfare in Print)
Administration: Anthea Kirk and Hannah Robson
Photos on back cover
Top: Mattie, photo provided by Andrea Bratt Frick (story on page 116)
Middle: Rocio and Jack, photo provided by Rocio Fonseca (story on page 142)
Bottom: Darbi, photo provided by Kim Lopes (story on page 1)

The book trade distributors
Australia: Bookwise International
Canada: Publishers Group Canada
New Zealand: Addenda Publishing
United Kingdom: Airlift Book Company
United States of America: Publishers Group West

The legal details
First published 2006
ISBN-10: 0-9582571-0-8
ISBN-13: 978-0-9582-5710-7
SMARTER than JACK is a trademark of Avocado Press Limited
Copyright © 2006 Avocado Press Limited

Contents

Responsible animal care

The stories in this book have been carefully reviewed to ensure that they do not promote the mistreatment of animals in any way.

It is important to note, however, that animal care practices can vary substantially from country to country, and often depend on factors 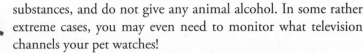 such as climate, population density, predators, disease control, local by-laws and social norms. Animal care practices can also change considerably over time; in some instances, practices considered perfectly acceptable many years ago are now considered unacceptable.

Therefore, some of the stories in this book may involve animals in situations that are not normally condoned in your community. We strongly advise that you consult with your local animal welfare charity if you are in any way unsure about the best way to look after animals in your care.

You may also find, when reading these stories, that you can learn from other people's (often unfortunate) mistakes. We also advise that you take care to ensure your pet does not eat poisonous plants or other dangerous substances, and do not give any animal alcohol. In some rather extreme cases, you may even need to monitor what television channels your pet watches!

Creating your SMARTER than JACK

Smart Rescued Animals is a special book that shows how remarkable those animals who have been rescued from adversity are. It also celebrates the amazing individuals and animal welfare charities that rescue them.

Thank you so much to everyone who submitted stories, especially those who had a story selected as this provided the content for this wonderful book. Many others, too, had a hand in the book's creation; you will see their names throughout these pages.

The people at the participating animal welfare charities assisted us greatly too, and were wonderful to work with. Profit from sales will help these animal welfare charities in their admirable quest to improve animal welfare.

Thanks to bookstores for making this book widely available to our readers, and thanks to readers for purchasing this book and for enjoying it and for giving it to others as gifts.

We hope you enjoy *Smart Rescued Animals* – and we hope that many animals and people benefit from it.

Jenny Campbell, creator of SMARTER than JACK

The delightful illustrations

The illustrations at the bottom of this book's pages are the work of Amanda Dickson. Amanda (27) is the human retainer and devotee of her Balinese cat Miss Tilburnia Cairo Casbah (9).

When not serving Miss Tilburnia, Amanda can be found reading, watching films and, most often, drawing. Amanda is a trained cartoon animator with four years' experience in the field who has now turned her hand to book illustration.

Amanda can be contacted by email at mandsmail@gmail.com.

Connecting animal lovers worldwide

Our readers and story contributors love to share their experiences and adventures with other like-minded people. So, to help them along, our books have some special features.

You can write direct to many of the contributors about your experiences with the animals in your life. Some contributors have included their contact details with their story. If an email address is given and you don't have access to the internet, just write a letter and send it via us and we'll be happy to send it on.

There are other ways you can be involved with SMARTER than JACK – tell us about an amazing animal charity in your community, a smart person you know, your questions about animals' behaviour or your favourite story in this book, or send us a photo of your animal with a SMARTER than JACK book. We also welcome your letters for our 'Your say' section. Our address details are on page 148.

Since 2002 the popular SMARTER than JACK series has helped raise over NZ$400,000 for animal welfare charities. It is now helping animals in Canada, the United States of America, Australia, New Zealand and the United Kingdom.

The future of the SMARTER than JACK series holds a number of exciting books – there will be ones about companion animals and intuitive animals. You can subscribe to the series now too.

If you've had an amazing encounter with a special animal we'd love to read about it. Story submission information is on page 147. You may also like to sign up to receive the Story of the Week for a bit of inspiration – visit www.smarterthanjack.com.

Foreword

When I wrote my book about the emotional lives of animals, *When Elephants Weep*, in 1995, it was the first popular book on this topic since Darwin's *The Expression of the Emotions in Man and Animals* was published in 1872. Science had ignored this fascinating field for over a hundred years.

Yet when I appeared before groups of people who lived with animals in their homes, they seemed dumbfounded that anybody would question the idea of animals' emotions. Of course animals had feelings! Had they not seen love in the eyes of their cats, dogs, rabbits, birds and even companion rats (who, I learned, were capable of great affection)?

As I toured America and other countries lecturing (but really listening to compelling stories), what struck me the most were tales about rescued animals who showered gratitude on their human rescuers, similar to the stories you will read in this book. (I defy you to read about the tribulations of Houston Humane Society's Burnie on page 101 without choking up.)

You cannot walk through a shelter without having your heart broken. The animals seem to know (why pretend – they definitely know) that you are their best chance for happiness. They know that in order to convince you to take them home they must touch your heart. Some animals do this literally, by reaching through the bars of their cages and tapping you with a soft paw. Other animals simply plead with their eyes, and the eloquent message is unmistakable: 'Please take me home. I will pay you back with unconditional love.'

I find the complexity of this behaviour astounding, and rich in implications. Could an argument be made that such behaviour is fake – just a show? I find it difficult to imagine any animal *pretending* to like you. Dogs seem incapable of such emotional deception, bestowing love even on those who mistreat them, and a cat wouldn't bother to hide his or her dislike. But even if we were to concede that the behaviour was somehow all an act, that in itself would be a remarkable achievement.

There are some scholars who claim that animals cannot form an image of the future. But these shelter animals 'see' themselves in a loving home. Even more astonishing is that they seem to know that, should they fail to convince you to adopt them, their future is bleak. This awareness of their fate is all too evident and heartbreaking. My mentor, the late Donald Griffin of Harvard University, wrote *The Question of Animal Awareness* in 1975. For him and for me, there is no question.

One thing I have learned from conversations with other animal devotees is how important animal rescue is. I now make a habit of telling all my audiences to visit a shelter or a rescue organisation when they are looking for an animal companion. There are so many animals who have been abandoned, abused or neglected and are desperate for the security of a loving home. In return they will show you their intelligence, warmth and rich emotions, especially their capacity for compassion. Each of you gives the other a precious gift. What greater happiness can any of us aspire to?

Dr Jeffrey Moussaieff Masson

About Jeffrey Masson

Dr Jeffrey Moussaieff Masson is a former psychoanalyst and director of the Freud Archives. He has written many books about the emotional lives of animals, including the international best-sellers *When Elephants Weep*, *Dogs Never Lie about Love* and *The Nine Emotional Lives of Cats*. Recently he published *The Pig Who Sang to the Moon* and *Raising the Peaceable Kingdom*.

He lives on Karaka Bay Beach in Auckland, New Zealand with his wife Leila, their sons Manu and Ilan, and three cats, Moko, Megala and Tamaiti.

1

Rescued animals find solutions

Darbi the wonder dog

photo
p73

We have a wonderful dog called Darbi whom we got from the Humane Society. She is beautiful but not very well trained. She can sit and give a paw when she sees a treat, and will go into her cage when told to. But she can't fetch, come or perform any other commands a trained dog of her age normally can. She has a habit of jumping on everyone to get love and attention, which sometimes scares the neighbourhood children.

One day we were out in the backyard with some of the neighbours. The kids were in the pool playing with a ball, when someone missed a catch and the ball went over the side and rolled under the deck. The deck was too low for the kids to reach under and retrieve it.

Darbi was lying quietly and observing the situation. Suddenly she got up, went under the deck and nosed the ball out to the edge so that the kids could get it! We were amazed. She was hero of the day, and the kids thought she was the smartest dog on the block.

By Kim Lopes, Almonte, Ontario, Canada

A good hiding place

photo p74

After travelling for three years, my fiancé Mick and I decided to settle in the Pilbara, Western Australia for work. There is a local animal rescue group called SAFE (Saving Animals From Euthanasia) which is always seeking 'foster parents' to look after abandoned pets until a full-time home can be found for them. It is something I had wanted to do for some time, as we were not really in a position to have a 'full-time' pet and I thought fostering would be a good compromise.

Our first 'foster child' was a ten-month-old kelpie cross called Chevy. She had been surrendered by her owners because she used to dig holes in the garden and tear up their irrigation system. I was a little apprehensive about fostering her, as we only have a small courtyard and were in the process of trying to establish a garden. But she needed a home so we agreed to give it a go. Mick wasn't too keen on the idea, but within in a week he and Chevy were best mates – until holes started appearing in his garden!

We came up with a solution and bought a kids' clamshell sandpit. We filled it with beach sand and encouraged her to dig in it and bury her bones there, and it actually worked! After a few weeks we couldn't imagine our lives without her, so we officially adopted her. Chevy has now been a full-time member of our family for six months and hasn't dug any holes since – well, not in the garden at any rate ...

One night we had some friends round for a barbeque. I had given Chevy a shin bone before I left for work that morning and she had obviously buried it in 'her spot'. Our friends had brought their dog over to play and Chevy was getting quite agitated about her bone possibly being discovered. She dug it up and was trying to find another spot to hide it. As she went slinking past, Mick said, 'Hide it good, girl, and don't let them find it.'

She obviously found a good hiding place, as she was soon back and playing with our friends' dog. We all had our tea and our guests left, so it was time to clean up and go to bed. About 4 am I was woken by the sound of my fiancé screaming, and then threatening all kinds of horrible things to his beloved dog. I turned on the light and was horrified to discover that she had taken her daddy's advice and had indeed found a good spot to bury her bone – right under his pillow!

By Justine O'Leary, Wickham, Western Australia

Clever Whiskey

photo p74

My mother got Whiskey from the SPCA when he was a kitten. She called him Whiskey because of his long multicoloured fur in shades of brown and amber. When she got him, the SPCA people said that he and his litter mate had been found in a sack on the riverbank. I guess someone had taken them down there to throw them in and decided not to – or, worse, thrown them off the bridge and missed the water.

Whiskey has always been a strange cat. He plods around slowly as if his feet weigh a ton, and sometimes gets a fright when you approach him even though he's the friendliest cat you'll ever meet. He loves to be picked up and carried around like a baby, but if you sit down he'll jump out of your arms.

We have a water dish in the kitchen for our cats, and one day we noticed that Whiskey kept dipping one of his paws into the water, then quickly retracting it and shaking water all over the lino. We usually have a wet spot on the floor in the kitchen because now he does this every time he has a drink.

3

Recently, we started having a closer look at Whiskey. If you catch him in a certain light you can see that one of his eyes reflects the light much more than the other one – we think that he must be at least half-blind. It was a revelation, as it explained all of Whiskey's strange behaviour. He gets a fright if you approach from his blind side, he likes to be carried because then he doesn't have to look where he's going, and he walks slowly so that he doesn't walk into anything. The reason he puts his paw into the water bowl is to get the water moving so that he can see where the water level is.

Of course, we love him all the more for his disability – and for his clever drinking technique.

By Gina Sturkenboom, Hamilton, New Zealand

Write to me … ✉
Email Gina
gas4@waikato.ac.nz

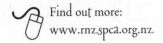 Find out more:
www.rnzspca.org.nz

A most wonderful decision

We rescued our gentle buff-coloured cocker spaniel Penny from a very sad situation. The woman we bought her from was actually living in a ten by ten foot kennel with about 20 dogs. Obviously, this was a disturbing situation for both the dogs and her. The dogs, all cocker spaniels, were caged and in various stages of growth, from newborn litters to older dogs.

Penny was kept in a very small, low cage with three other large dogs. She was only eight weeks old and was being trampled. Every instinct told me, my husband and daughter to leave without an animal, but we couldn't. Those spaniel eyes and that mischievous face wouldn't let us leave without her.

What a wonderful decision it was. Penny has given back to our family threefold in love, companionship and laughter. She has an adoring relationship with our granddaughters, Emily and Abby, who are 11 and seven years old respectively. Both girls love to have her participating in their fun, and she is quick to follow them around no matter what they are doing.

On one occasion Penny was at a sleepover at our daughter's home. The girls were upstairs playing with stuffed animals. Penny came downstairs, found her beloved stuffed pink pig and returned to the girls with her own well-worn toy. She obviously didn't want to be left out of playtime with her buddies!

I like to think that all three girls are fast friends and have learned a lot from each other: love, patience, fun and laughter.

By Donna Graham, Kanata,
Ontario, Canada

Write to me …

Email Donna
donna_112000@yahoo.com

Smart and sensitive

Anna was the smallest of a litter of kittens when I found her. I was ten years old and at a night game of cricket that my dad was playing.

My brothers and I were exploring the old toilets at the far end of the fields when we heard some kittens meowing. The whole litter had been dumped in the locked toilets. They were tiny and scrawny. It took us two hours, using milk and the smell of sausages, to coax the kittens out. They were all still too small to eat the sausages.

All of them came out except Anna. She was very small and, probably because of her current circumstances, not very trusting of humans. It was heartbreaking, but we had to leave her there alone that night. First thing in the morning we got the keys to the toilet block from the groundskeeper and drove down to rescue her.

Anna grew to be the most intelligent cat I'd ever had. She could open all the doors and windows, letting herself in and out. She worked out the cupboard door, and helped herself to the dried food if we didn't feed her on time!

Next to us, her greatest love was the heater. We had a gas heater where you had to push down and hold the buttons for it to light. My favourite memory is of watching Anna lift the latch where the buttons were, then proceed to place all her weight on her front paws and push down on the buttons in an attempt to light the heater.

Anna was also very sensitive. If ever someone in the family was sick or upset she would spend the night on their bed. Once when my younger brother was ill with a fever she woke my mother and took her in to check on him.

Sadly, we lost our clever Anna a few years ago. She is greatly missed, and I haven't come across a smarter or more sensitive animal since.

By Elizabeth Wheeler, North Parramatta, New South Wales, Australia

The dog who trained himself

In 1946 I got a job on a sheep farm, having worked for a year on a dairy farm. I had only one dog, Faye, to take with me. As this was not really satisfactory, I asked a drover if he had any spare dogs to sell me. He said, 'You can have this useless one for nothing if you like, he's 12 months old and hasn't done a scrap of work.'

So, for the sake of appearances, I took Scott as well. Shortly after I'd started my new job he began working and, without any training, became a very useful heading-cum-huntaway. When I had to shift sheep through a paddock already stocked with sheep, he would go (on command) out into the paddock and scatter the sheep out of the way for me and then help keep my mob together on the way through.

Then, when I was moving my mob of ewes and lambs along a roadway, I could send him down the side of the mob and stop him with one whistle when he was almost at the front. He would bark and then trot back towards me, barking occasionally, which was great to keep the mob moving along. At that stage of my career I really knew nothing about training dogs, so what could have been better for me than a dog who could train himself!

By Tim Suckling, Katikati,
New Zealand

Write to me ... ✉
Email Tim
timiris@orcon.net.nz

Fergus the fishing cat

Fergus was nestled snugly into an old biscuit carton when he arrived in the remote hydro village along with the weekly groceries. He was destined to be the resident cat at the hostel situated next door to our house. Unfortunately, the residents lost interest in him and Fergus was in dire need of a new home or a sad fate awaited him. A young family living further up the hill offered to adopt him. However, after several days of their feeding him and then having him head back down to play with our cats, we gave him a home with us.

Fergus developed the habit of following our schoolboy son down to the river to go eeling. When an eel was caught, he was always a close spectator. He would wait for it to be skinned, as he would often be given a tasty morsel.

7

After our son had departed for boarding school, we began finding small eels and the odd trout lying on the back doormat. We could only presume that Fergus had gone fishing on his own. The night staff at the power station confirmed our suspicions. During the night the power station was shut down and so the river level fell considerably, exposing rocks and pools that were usually covered by rushing water. Fergus was spotted leaping from rock to rock and, every now and then, making a grab into one of the pools with his paw.

Then one morning, instead of the usual tiny fish on the doorstep, there sat a very bedraggled Fergus. His fur was wet and matted with slime, and he reeked of fish.

It took a considerable amount of warm soapy water to restore him to his usual cuddly self. We can only imagine what took place, but we reckon he would have had a marvellous 'the one that got away' story to tell. We are not sure whether it was the confrontation with the eel or the indignity of being washed in the sink, but his fishing expeditions came to an abrupt end.

By Catherine Palmer, Ashburton,
New Zealand

Write to me … ✉
Email Catherine
BLCJ@xtra.co.nz

One determined dog

I'd just finished packing for a weekend away when Jess, a blue heeler cross, arrived at the farm on the back of a ute with four yapping siblings. The foreman's wife was choosing a pup for her son. As I watched, the pups came rolling out of the dust behind a visiting Dalmatian. But only one of them kept following the Dalmatian, actually heeling the bigger dog.

Photo provided by Maggie Perry

Jess takes a well-deserved rest

I caught the pup as she ran past and turned her onto her back. She fought like a grounded eel to get all four paws back on terra firma. Then she was off after the Dalmatian again. Seeing so much determination in such a small package made my mind up. I ran and told my husband Brian that she'd be drowned if we didn't take her, and so we became proud owners of a very vocal pup.

When she was about four months old we moved to a cotton farm on the Queensland/New South Wales border, and Jess would come out to work with me.

One day, when she was about eight months old, Jess didn't follow her usual routine of running up and down the paddocks in the shallow water that ran down the furrows. Instead, she stood on the bank barking at me. I had to finish the run of opening and closing the pipes before I could go and see what was bothering her. She was standing over what appeared from a distance to be a bundle of rags.

As I got closer I saw that it was moving a bit – it was a pup. I bundled the pup into a towel that I carried in the truck and took him up to the workshop, where the lads informed me it was vermin – a red fox cub. As the pup was grey, I hadn't realised he was a fox.

One of the girls took him in and Basil survived to go on to a wildlife farm, where he now educates people on the vermin introduced to Australia. Chalk one up to Jess.

A few months later, I got a call from one of the lads to go back to my house. There was one of my neighbour Heather's chickens on its back on the front lawn, and next to it lay Jess. She sat up as I got closer and studied me. Looking at the chook, I could see that it was alive but stunned, so I carried it over to Heather with Jess trotting at my heels, whining softly.

Heather's first words were a relief to me. 'Goanna. I've been looking for this bird's nest for weeks, but she's been hiding from me down by the river.' The goanna (a large Australian lizard) had either chewed the back of the chicken's neck to move her or lifted her off his feast of eggs by the back of her neck, and she'd gone into shock. Jess had found her and brought her home. Chalk two up to Jess.

All of this had happened 15 years ago. On the day that Jess could no longer walk up the hill and Brian had to carry her to the vet's, I remembered it all.

On March 15, 2006 – aged 16, deaf, losing her eyesight, losing the use of her strong back and hind legs, and having no control over her functions – she gave me a look that said, *Let me go*. She was embarrassed, sore and sad. A proud animal with the kindest eyes, softest heart and most wicked sense of humour, Jess went to sleep for the last time. She was more than ready, and she chose that day to be her last.

I want to commemorate her as a loyal, loving and remarkable dog who almost never had the chance to save foxes and chickens. I remember watching that puppy heeling the Dalmatian, and I know that the determination she showed then to do her best never left her.

Missing you, Jess.

By Maggie Perry, Gold Coast, Queensland, Australia

2

Rescued animals show they care

Doctor Sasha

We have two dogs, Sasha and her son BJ, whom we rescued from a very miserable existence. They have become loving and loyal companions to us and to each other.

One evening, BJ started making sounds like he was gasping for air. He is only a young dog so we immediately thought he might have got something caught in his throat or wedged in his mouth, as he is always stealing food – a trait stemming from extended periods of neglect and starvation.

When he calmed down I checked his mouth, but it was all clear. A short time later he started gasping again. This time he seemed more distressed. We decided to make an emergency dash to the after-hours vet but, before we could get him into the car, the gasping stopped and he was breathing normally once again.

BJ had a few more gasping episodes, which passed quickly and then he seemed okay. But something was still worrying him as he was reluctant to sleep in his bed, so he snuggled down on a rug at the foot of our bed.

Soon after midnight BJ started gasping again. This time his mother Sasha was close at hand. She started making a similar noise and nudging me. I realised that the sound she was making was with her nose, so I immediately started massaging down both sides of BJ's nose. Very soon he was able to give several snorts and then he calmed down. After several minutes of massage, BJ got up and went to his own bed, obviously confident that he wasn't going to get distressed any more. He must have had something stuck up his nose that was now cleared.

My first thought was that Sasha had been jealous of the attention BJ was getting, but then I realised that, as soon as I'd focused my attention on his nose, she'd stopped making the gasping noise and gone back to bed. She has always been a very special little dog, but I was so amazed at the way she showed me how to help her son.

By Barbara Bryan, Lower Hutt, New Zealand

Cricket the Christmas feral

My husband had trapped Cricket, his litter mates and their mother on the dunes. The cat family were starving as there was no summer garbage to eat. No more kind people to leave out food. Mice were getting more difficult for the young mother to catch to feed her hungry brood.

It took a week to get them all safely to the animal shelter. Back then we didn't understand what a stressful environment a shelter is for any animal. Torn away from familiar surroundings, siblings or their people, they grieve, don't eat, get depressed and, too often, fall sick and die. With cage after cage of animals, one sneeze starts everyone snivelling. Yet this was Cricket's best chance.

As Christmas approached, Cricket started sneezing. Each day, when my husband stopped at the shelter to check on the little family, he appeared sicker. His prospects didn't look good, so we decided to bring him and his medicine home for some TLC.

That first night we took turns holding him, cleaning his nose and forcing food, water and medicine into him. Cricket finally slept wrapped in a towel on my husband's chest. By morning he was noticeably better. He continued to improve daily; however, now his sisters were sick. As the shelter was closing to prevent holiday adoptions that often turned into returned animals, we took them and their mother too. They were our Christmas gift to each other.

And Cricket was quite a present. He grew into a plain brown cat with a solid muscular body and irregular white markings. But there was nothing plain about his sweet temperament.

Several months later his sister Annie, confined to a cage after being spayed, was crying inconsolably. Softly chirring, Cricket approached the cage, slipped his paws through the bars and cradled her until she was soothed into silence. When she was calm, he sat back on his haunches, keeping one arm draped around her. He remained nearby, until she could be released from the cage several days later.

Cricket has been a Christmas gift that keeps on giving. He's a special little feral who enriched our lives and stole our hearts.

By Madelyn Filipski, Cape May Court House, New Jersey, United States of America

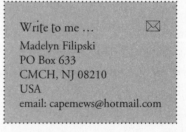

Write to me …

Madelyn Filipski
PO Box 633
CMCH, NJ 08210
USA
email: capemews@hotmail.com

Thank you for rescuing me

On the day we moved into our new house, we were asked if we would take a German shepherd/English bull terrier cross into our care. She was about ten months old, black with a white blaze on her

13

chest, collarless and starving – and the police were going to have her destroyed. How could we say no? We called her Roma, because she had been found roaming.

The problem was that we already had a little silver tabby called Dinky, who had just had kittens. We were worried that, when we introduced Roma to Dinky, World War III was going to break out! But as soon as they met they became friends and sat by the fire together. Roma helped Dinky to wash the kittens, wagging her tail and enjoying every minute of it.

Roma's relationship with Dinky and the kittens was one thing, but with us she was so disobedient that we nearly gave up. However we fought on, giving Roma love and attention, and scolding her when necessary. She became a wonderful pet.

When we were expecting our first baby, some people suggested that we have Roma put down. They said that, since we made Roma feel like such an important part of the family, she might kill the child out of jealousy. But we would not consider it – we simply could not envisage life without her.

We let Roma get used to all the baby's things as we prepared for the birth. When we brought little David home, we put him in his pram and called Roma over to inspect the new arrival. She sniffed, got all excited, and then sat by the pram as if to guard its contents.

Roma was a good nursemaid. As David grew, she would lie upside down on the floor and let him put bricks on her tummy, then she would roll over and let them all fall off. This game would be repeated many times, accompanied by David's shrieks of laughter. She would also sit by his pram on guard duty. If anyone strayed near her front end she was all snarls, but her rear end was wagging like mad.

Dinky had another litter, and during the birth she let Roma wash and tend each new arrival. One day we couldn't find Dinky or the kittens anywhere. After searching for a while, we noticed that Roma hadn't moved from her kennel on the back porch. She was lying there with her head on her paws, looking out of the kennel doorway with an 'I know something you don't' smile on her face. We lifted up the top of the kennel, and there were Dinky and the kittens curled up in the back, with Roma on guard.

We are so glad that we ignored the advice of others who didn't know the temperament of our beloved dog. Perhaps the devotion she showed us was her way of saying, *Thank you for rescuing me.*

By Gwen Keene, Upper Hutt, New Zealand

The tailless wonder

Rafferty was a golden retriever who had been neglected. He had also been burned and had his tail cut off. When he came to me he had a fungal infection all over his skin, and had to be shaved so that we could treat it. There was conflict between Raf and another dog in his original adoptive family as they would not separate the two dogs at feeding times, so Raf was returned to the closest foster home – me. Before I got him in my door, I was in love with him.

Raf was very gentle, and could be walked on the thinnest show leash. He helped out with all my foster dogs. I could put a leash in his mouth and he would walk another dog. If other dogs started a dispute, he would get in the middle with a low bark and stop the conflict. He loved loud noises. While the other dogs cowered, he would stand on the porch with me and watch lightning or fireworks.

When a foster Labrador, Rosa, delivered 12 puppies at our house, Rafferty walked into the pen and then sniffed and licked each one of the pups. Eventually Rosa was adopted into our family, and she and Rafferty remained close friends.

15

Photo provided by Karen Golab

Gentle Rafferty

A friend approached me about starting a pet therapy programme with Rafferty. He was tested and received his certification. We started visiting nursing homes, hospitals and schools. I could let Raf go in a crowd of people without fear that he would wander off or hurt anyone. At one of the schools, there was a little girl who rarely spoke. Right from our first visit the little girl and Raf formed a special bond, and she started talking more as time went on.

When I least expected it, Rafferty was diagnosed with Hemangiosarcoma, a form of canine cancer. For months we tried various forms of chemotherapy, gradually reducing the dose because the side effects were too severe. Finally, Rafferty collapsed in my kitchen one night and I rushed him to the vet, who stayed after hours to see him. Once she'd examined him, we decided his time had come. Surrounding Rafferty with caring people – the vet, two vet technicians, my husband, me and my little girl, all of us in tears – we let him go.

My family has been involved in rescue for more than 13 years. Over 500 dogs and the occasional cat have come and gone from our lives. But never have we been sadder to lose a dog than we were when Rafferty died. He left a huge hole in our hearts and our home.

By Karen Golab, St. Peters, Missouri, United States of America

The pigeon and the cat

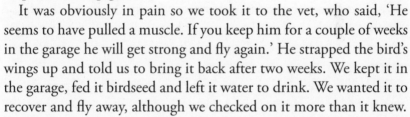

About 20 years ago, my late husband brought me the strangest surprise ever: a pigeon.

It was obviously in pain so we took it to the vet, who said, 'He seems to have pulled a muscle. If you keep him for a couple of weeks in the garage he will get strong and fly again.' He strapped the bird's wings up and told us to bring it back after two weeks. We kept it in the garage, fed it birdseed and left it water to drink. We wanted it to recover and fly away, although we checked on it more than it knew.

By the time we returned to the vet, *it* had become *him* and he had a name, Homeboy. The vet undid the strapping and said that he should fly away in another couple of days. However, the wing dropped and Homeboy was walking on it, making it bleed. This time the vet said, 'He will either have to be put down or his wing will have to be removed.' There was no way we would let him be put down, so Homeboy had the amputation and came home to spend the rest of his life with us.

He had to live indoors as it was becoming cold at night. The problem was that we had a cat, Ludo. She was a rescued cat and very spoiled indeed, and we wondered just how we could cope with both a cat and a wild bird in the house. Our first job was to convert a reject kitchen cabinet into a cage. We stood this on a television stand on wheels to keep Homeboy away from Ludo.

Homeboy's first night was spent in his new cage, with Ludo close by – his injured wing probably smelled very good to her! We thought

17

it would never work, but Ludo got used to Homeboy and they lived happily together for seven years. Ludo always gave in to Homeboy; she was a remarkable cat and lived until she was 21.

They would have differences of opinion sometimes, especially when Ludo wanted the best place by the fire. Homeboy always pushed her out of the way, and in fact, when we moved and had a gas fire with imitation coals, Homeboy would not let Ludo near it at all!

Ludo accepted Homeboy as part of the family. After a while we were able to go out and leave them together in the house. In all the years we had Homeboy, Ludo never hurt him at all. She was very gentle – unlike Homeboy, who attacked everyone who came to the house.

We had a wonderful time with our cat and pigeon. Whoever said cats and birds can't get along should have seen our two together. They could have taught some humans a few things.

By Carol King, Swindon, Wiltshire, England

Boris the guardian cat

When I moved to Napier I made some great new friends, of both the two-legged and the four-legged variety. One friend, Amanda, introduced me to her feline companions, which included her wonderful cat Boris.

For some time, Boris – a long-haired moggie stray cat – had been sneaking through the cat door and trying to pinch Buffy's food (Buffy is Amanda's other cat). As the days passed, Boris, Buffy and Amanda got to know each other well.

Boris came in one day in bad condition. He'd been in a fight which resulted in an abscess/infection and pain. After a trip to the vet, together with antibiotics and TLC, Amanda nursed Boris back to health. Buffy and Amanda decided to adopt Boris.

But the story doesn't end there.

Each work day, Amanda walks to the end of her street and then round the corner to the bus stop. She began to notice Boris following her. When they reached the bus stop, Boris would sit next to Amanda and wait with her for the bus. Once the bus had arrived and Amanda got on and the bus departed, Boris would make his way home.

When Amanda arrived back at the bus stop later in the day, Boris would be sitting there waiting for his friend. This little 'guardian cat' with a courageous and loyal heart accompanies Amanda – his friend and owner – home.

Amanda saved Boris from a life of being a stray, abandoned on the streets, and in return he escorts her round. He is a loyal companion and friend/soulmate.

Here's to you, Boris!

By Wildspirit, Napier, Hawkes Bay, New Zealand

A diamond in the rough

I foster dogs for our local animal shelter, and Sheba originally came to me as a foster dog. She is part Rottweiler and they didn't have a place to keep her. After one look into her eyes I knew she wasn't leaving my house – it was love. However, I had no idea of the work this love would involve me in over the next several months.

When I got Sheba she was between six and eight months old and weighed about 50 pounds. She was so scared of people she would roll over and wet herself when you reached down to her. She wasn't housebroken and it took us four months to trust her not to mess on

19

the floor. She would tear up things when left by herself. She was so scared she would stick to me like glue, and sometimes would even hold onto me with her paws so that I wouldn't leave her.

Sheba is now about two and a half years old and weighs about 93 pounds. With love and patience she has become the cleanest dog I have ever seen. At 15 months old she became totally trustworthy when left alone in the house.

But the best part of this story is how she acts towards my other foster dogs – she really is their hero. For the pups, she is like a surrogate mother, sleeping beside them and protecting them by putting her body between them and other dogs. For the young dogs, she is a teacher. Whenever I get a young dog who is not housebroken, she helps me train them. She goes outside with them, waits for them to go, then shows them the way back to the door. She also makes them feel at home by teaching them how to play. She gets a pull-toy and sticks it in a young dog's mouth until the dog takes it. If the other dog gets too rough she pokes it with her nose as if to say, *Settle down now*, and then starts the game over.

I cannot believe how much easier she has made dog fostering for me. By making my foster dogs more comfortable around other dogs, she helps them become well adjusted and more adoptable. In doing this she has helped to save a lot of dogs and puppies. I couldn't have done half as much without her – together we have fostered over 20 dogs and pups.

Sheba is my superdog, best friend and partner in rescuing, training, and rehoming abandoned dogs. She means everything to me and I love her more every day. She is one of the smartest dogs I know. So, next time you are looking for a dog, I want you to consider shelter dogs. You never know when you will find a dog as great as mine – a real diamond in the rough who has turned out to be priceless.

By Jo-Ann Livingstone, Port Howe, Nova Scotia, Canada

A true friend

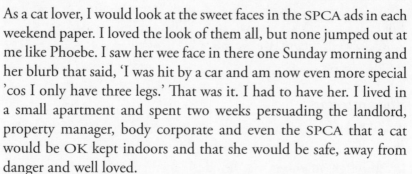

As a cat lover, I would look at the sweet faces in the SPCA ads in each weekend paper. I loved the look of them all, but none jumped out at me like Phoebe. I saw her wee face in there one Sunday morning and her blurb that said, 'I was hit by a car and am now even more special 'cos I only have three legs.' That was it. I had to have her. I lived in a small apartment and spent two weeks persuading the landlord, property manager, body corporate and even the SPCA that a cat would be OK kept indoors and that she would be safe, away from danger and well loved.

Finally I brought my girl home. Phoebe took to apartment life quickly. She enjoyed everything about it, except one thing: men. I lived in the apartment with two other girls and, needless to say, boyfriends and other male friends would come round quite often. Every time, Phoebe would be most put out and hide. We thought that maybe it was a man who had been driving the car that hit her, causing her to lose her leg, and she wasn't about to forgive whoever had done that to her. Whatever the case, she was not a fan of men in general and would be extra sweet to us if one of us was upset by one of the men in our lives.

One night, not long after she moved in with us, I'd had yet another fight with a boyfriend. I was sitting on my bed, sobbing, and Phoebe was most concerned. She kept making soothing chirping noises and looking at me intently. Suddenly it became too much and she rushed over to me, chirping loudly, and began licking up my tears.

From that moment I realised I had made a friend for life. She has been there for me time and time again, and will be for as long as she lives. We are very close these days. She now respects my choices in boyfriends and male friends – although she is a little aloof towards them to begin with, as if warning them that *she* is what's important to me and men will come and go but she will be there till the end. I am in perfect agreement with her.

By Sarah McIntosh, Wellington, New Zealand

The protectors

As wildlife carers, we come into contact every day with animals that show amazing resilience to pain and fear, as well as a strong will to live through anything that life deals to them. Not quite as often, though, we also get to see the amazing bravery these wild animals have.

We got a call to go and pick up an injured bird – a tawny frogmouth who had apparently fallen from a tree and damaged his wing. He was lying on the ground with his wing spread out at a peculiar angle, and being attacked by other wildlife. While we assessed the situation, the female of the pair, obviously very distressed, started swooping at us from above. This was a completely natural and expected reaction.

It was only when we went to pick up the male that we realised there was a young chick under his wing. The 'injured' male flew up and also started to attack us from the air. All along, it had been the chick who had fallen out of the nest, and the male had been protecting his baby on the ground while his partner protected them both from the air.

We think this is an amazing and heart-warming story which shows that animals do have emotions. This seems all too often to be forgotten – especially by the small number of us who grumble about wild animals intruding into our lives. Wild animals probably feel exactly the same way about us.

By Lyn Robson and Sue Penfold, Western Australia

3

Rescued animals outwit us

The biscuit ghost

Seven years ago, I spent a day looking for a kitten. I was at the last home I was to visit that day, and the guy there took me round the back to where the kittens were. And there she was – this sad, scrawny little puppy chained to the house tap, with dirt stuck to her coat. Her eyes followed us, but her head stayed on the ground between her paws.

We went into the garage and I looked at the kittens, but none of them was the right one. As we walked out of the garage, the puppy sat up. Immediately, the guy yelled at her and told her to lie down. I had never seen a dog cower so quickly – she was so sad it made my stomach ache. Her owner said that he wasn't looking for a new home for her. I was about to give him my contact details in case he changed his mind, when he said I could have her for $60. I couldn't really afford it, but I had no hesitation in handing over the money. I scooped her up and ran to the car.

The vet said she was okay on basic health but, from the condition she was in, she had practically been starved. It took a good few weeks of steady feeding for her to gain weight. We named her Tess. She bloomed, bounced and became the happiest puppy – so full of life. My other dog loved her and played mother to her from the moment she arrived. She was family.

Sadly, Tess had been with us for only a year when she contracted parvovirus and passed away. I believe I was meant to find her, and give her the family, the care and the love that she deserved.

I have many memories of her funny antics. The one that makes me laugh the most was her 'biscuit habit'. Packets of biscuits used to go missing from the cupboard. For weeks, I growled at my children for eating them. They swore they hadn't, but there was no other explanation I could think of. In the end I thought I must be going crazy, until one night when I had drinks with my neighbour, who shed some light on the situation.

She explained that, as soon as I drove down the drive and out the gate, Tess would run round to the back of the house. If I wasn't going to be away for too long, I would leave the back door open for the dogs. My neighbour would see Tess return to the front lawn with a packet of biscuits. Tess would carefully open one end and shake the packet so they would all fall out, and then she and my other dog would eat them. Sometimes she would go back for another packet, sometimes it was just the one. Well, you can imagine how I laughed as I was sure that my neighbour was having me on, but we put it to the test.

I went home and got into the car. I backed down the drive and parked just up the road, then ran back next door. We stood in my neighbour's kitchen looking out the window – and there was Tess, proudly trotting round the corner with a packet of biscuits in her mouth. I couldn't believe it! Sure enough, she carefully opened one end and then stood up and shook the packet to empty the contents onto the ground, whereupon both dogs ate the biscuits.

I tried to work out how she got into the cupboard as there were no handles, and the locks were an old type where you had to put your finger on and push the button as you pulled the door open ... to this day I still don't know how she did it – but she did.

I asked my neighbour how long she'd known about Tess's 'biscuit habit', and she said it had been going on for weeks. Why hadn't she told me? She thought it was the most talented, sneaky and cheeky thing she had ever seen! So, did I move the biscuits from the cupboard? No. Tess wasn't greedy, although she could have been – and when I had seen her doing it she'd looked so proud and happy with herself that I wasn't going to take those moments away from her. I also never growled at her or let her know she had been caught out.

I let Tess be who she was and, to this day, I have no regrets about that.

By Amelia Hunter, Auckland,
New Zealand

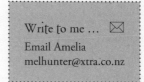

Write to me ...

Email Amelia
melhunter@xtra.co.nz

Intelligent genes

photo
p76

This story concerns a rat named Bumpus O'Beast, the son of my famous Blonde Mercedes (whom I consider to be the greatest rat of all time). Unfortunately for Bumpus, I made a poor judgement call and adopted him out to a very bad home. I had to move heaven and earth, but six months later I got him back.

There's one particularly memorable incident which demonstrates his intelligence. One day when I was in a hurry to go out, I decided to quickly sweep under the table that his cage was on using a hand-held dustpan. While I was all hunkered down I felt something hit my head. I looked up at the ceiling and could see nothing crumbling so I resumed sweeping. Then it happened again. This time when I

25

looked up, there was a pert pink nose and some black fuzz poking out from between the bars of the cage.

Sometimes I'm a little slow so I didn't immediately make the connection, but the third time it happened I stood bolt upright and caught the culprit red-handed, rolling a large block of rat chow towards me with his little pink human-like hands. I couldn't help but exclaim, 'Oh, it's you!'

In response to my voice, he dropped the block and started hopping up and down, skipping in a circle and doing what I can only interpret as 'the rat dance'. Other rat owners who have kept charismatic unneutered males might have seen variations of this fascinating behaviour.

I concluded that he had been dropping food on me to get my attention, since he had honed in on my exact position beneath the cage. He also 'taught' a second rat – supposedly the 'dumbest' rat in the cage – to imitate him. But what made Bumpus incredible was not the premeditated action of removing a block from the dispenser and rolling it along with his hands to my exact spot below the cage, but his reaction each time I caught his eye – the 'rat dance'. I could only interpret this as joy.

Bumpus went on to act in a short film, where he amazed the crew by responding to verbal instructions. He was also my inspiration for 'Bumpus Place', the animal rescue centre I have founded, due to his altruistic inclination to serve his fellow rats by cleaning, feeding and providing warmth for those who were sick or handicapped. Likewise, he made a habit of sleeping on the coldest parts of my body – my nose or toes – to warm them up at the expense of his own comfort.

Bumpus passed away in April 2005, but his daughter Sassafras recently showed the same kind of extraordinary intelligence by showering me with pellets from her litter box as I slept. This shows a lot of determination too, and was quite a feat considering the fact that she is partially paralysed. A camera hidden in my bed has since immortalised her genius.

By Charlotte Stanley, Mississauga, Ontario, Canada

Write to me ... ✉
Email Charlotte
squeekweek@yahoo.ca

Find out more:
www.geocities.com/squeekweek/
rescues

She knew what she wanted

When I first came to the country town where I now live, I stayed in a caravan park for a few months. The first night I was there, a stray tortie cat meowed at my caravan door for food but all I had to give her was a saucer of milk.

The next day when I came home from work, the tortie saw me as I walked through the park gate. But, instead of running towards me, she ran straight across the park to my caravan and waited there to greet me. I thought this showed intelligence. Needless to say, she got proper food from me from then on!

I adopted P'dl, as I called the cat, and had her spayed. She was only allowed inside the caravan while I was home. During the day she stayed outside.

A while later, I brought home a stray kitten from work. Because he was so little, I kept him inside the caravan during the day. P'dl seemed to absolutely hate the kitten for about a month, then one day when I came home and opened the caravan door, not only was the kitten inside but P'dl was there too. There was fly-wire hanging down over the bed, and I could see that she must have got under the skylight and then her weight had made the fly-wire collapse and

 27

she had fallen through onto the bed. (By the way, from then on she adored the kitten and came into milk and fed him, even though she had been spayed six months previously.)

However, I did not really want P'dl in the caravan all day, so the next morning before I left I closed the skylight completely. When I came home and opened the door, there she was inside again, with her now-adopted son. She had realised that fly-wire was not impenetrable and had pushed though the fly-wire in one of the windows. After that, I just left a window open for her.

P'dl lived with me for many years, finally dying of old age when she was about 23 years old.

By Jenifer Winterbine, Huntly, Victoria, Australia

A clever strategy

Our cat Blossom was found by my brother in the gutter of the main road. Only about three weeks old, she was way too young to be separated from her mother, but she thrived on love and infant formula. She would suck on everything, particularly shoelaces and blankets.

Blossom is a fluffy white blue-eyed cat who is completely deaf and has a somewhat unpleasant temperament. Although we are a family of cat lovers, Blossom likes only my mother, barely tolerates the rest of the immediate family, and growls, spits at and scratches everyone else (especially vets).

She is also a very clever cat. When my parents are going out, she is brought inside since her deafness makes her vulnerable to attacks from other cats. Also, as she is a white cat, it is best to protect her ears from the midday sun. However, she doesn't like being left inside alone and has come up with a strategy to avoid it.

What's Blossom planning now?

When she realises my parents are getting ready to go out, she gives them an unimpressed glare and then uses her litter tray. She's worked out that one of my parents will then take the tray outside to clean it before they go out. As soon as the back door is opened for them to do this, Blossom does her best to escape outside and hide. Her trickery has resulted in many delayed outings!

By Neri Baker, Castle Hill, New South Wales, Australia

Snoopy the rescued crow

Many years ago someone brought a baby crow to my sister, who was an animal rescuer. She nursed the baby until he was ready for release, but he refused to fly away. So, for 24 years, Snoopy lived with my sister and her family.

During this time Snoopy learned to say a few words, and people walking by the house would say hello and Snoopy would say hello to them. For his safety, my sister built a very large cage for him to sit in on the porch during the summer.

When Snoopy wanted his favourite treats, Cheez Doodles (baked corn snacks) and spaghetti, he would lie on the bottom of his cage with his feet in the air and scream, *HELP!*

One beautiful summer day a police car was passing my sister's house, when the two officers heard what sounded like a woman screaming for help. They jumped out of their car and raced to the house with guns drawn. Imagine my sister's surprise when she walked out the door to give Snoopy his treats and found two policemen staring into Snoopy's cage as he screamed, *HELP! HELP! HELP!*

By Diane Blakney, Fort Pierce,
Florida, United States of America

Write to me …

Diane Blakney
116 Gardenia Avenue
Fort Pierce, FL 34982
USA
email: dblakney@ircc.edu

Beware a cat bearing gifts

A couple of years ago, I ended up adopting my neighbours' kitten. I called her Bubba. It seemed to suit her as she was so little. She'd had a hard start to life, being only six months old, sporting half a tail and being pregnant at the time she moved in.

After Bubba had had her kittens, she started to bring me presents – mostly birds and insects. Why she didn't take them to her kittens I don't know. Maybe they were to thank me for feeding her family.

One morning, I heard her come into my bedroom. With all the noise she was making I knew she had a present for me. Not wanting to get up, I thought I'd just ignore her and clean up the mess later.

Well, Bubba had other ideas. She jumped up onto my bed and threw the poor bird at the wall so that it ricocheted onto my pillow and hit me on the head. As you can imagine, the bedroom erupted into chaos. I think she wanted me to appreciate her gift then, not later!

I still laugh about it to this day and can't imagine my life without her. I'm so pleased the neighbours left her behind.

By Leanne Hadwin, Hamilton, New Zealand

Quick to learn

When my son wanted a pet, we went to the RSPCA in search of a kitten. I fell in love with a little black tortoiseshell female who had a splash of colour on one side of her face, but my son liked the male ginger tabby he was holding. I felt I couldn't put the little tortoiseshell back now as she was curled up on my shoulder with her head resting against my neck, so we took both of them.

They settled in quickly and grew rapidly. The tortoiseshell, Shady, followed me everywhere. Shady was observant and curious, but I didn't realise how intelligent she was until one morning I went into the kitchen and heard a scrabbling noise in the walk-in pantry. As soon as I got close there was a thumping sound as something jumped down from one of the shelves. As the little cat ran out the pantry door, I realised she had chewed a hole in the bottom of the packet of dried cat food that I kept on the third shelf. The clever girl had figured out exactly where I kept her food! I rewarded her with a small handful of food, then put the packet in a different cupboard, above the refrigerator.

The next morning I was astounded to find Shady on top of the fridge trying to pull open the cupboard door where she knew her food was. She couldn't do it because the door opened outwards and

31

each time she got it open slightly it started to push her off the top of the fridge.

When we moved to a different house with sliding glass and screen doors, Shady quickly figured out how to open the doors by catching the edge with her claws and pulling it sideways until there was enough room to squeeze her head through. She would come and go as she pleased, but I could never get her to close the door! One day I even found her trying to pull up the bolt we used to lock the sliding door in the laundry, but she wasn't strong enough.

I was very upset when, as a result of a fight with a stray cat, Shady contracted feline Aids and eventually had to be put down. Whenever I think of how loving she was, how intelligent, and how quickly she worked out what she needed to know, it brings a smile to my face.

By John Litchen, Robina, Queensland, Australia

Find out more:
www.rspca.org.au

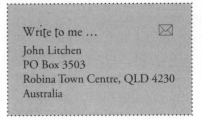

Write to me ... ✉

John Litchen
PO Box 3503
Robina Town Centre, QLD 4230
Australia

Elevator smarts

Cats have to be very smart to survive on the streets in Seoul. In Korean myth, cats are demons because their eyes glow in the dark, so Koreans rarely help a stray cat. However, the one I rescued was smart enough to survive on Seoul's city streets, and do it well.

When I found Sasha, she was digging through the garbage bags at the kerb to find food. She must have belonged to someone at some time because, when I came close, she let me touch her. She was white, plump and had two blotches of black fur along her back. The fact that she was heavy was unusual, and when I took her to the vet I learned she was pregnant. I couldn't return her to the streets, so I thought I'd see if she'd adjust to life in an apartment.

I needn't have worried. She settled into my two small rooms, and my life – and my heart – very quickly. She appreciated the regular food and having a clean, warm place to sleep, and she loved the attention I gave her.

But once the kittens were born and I'd located homes for them, she'd often sit on the windowsill, looking outside somewhat wistfully. She wasn't unhappy but she was clearly a little bored with four walls, so we developed a new routine. I'd mark students' papers for an hour in the evening, and then I'd take Sasha out to the grassy park behind the building for an hour. She'd play in the grass, and I'd read while I waited for her. When she was ready she'd follow me back indoors, usually quite willingly. The security guards at the desk would chuckle as we trooped in. The two of us then stood patiently waiting for the elevator doors to open and take us back up to the apartment.

The problem started towards the end of the semester. My marking load became substantially heavier and Sasha wasn't willing to wait the extra time it took each night. She wanted to go out. I started leaving the apartment door open so that she could roam the hall and visit the other teachers in their apartments. I thought that would keep her occupied and, on the first few nights I tried it, it did.

But one night it didn't. While I was immersed in my students' term papers, Sasha had had enough. She'd wandered the halls, she'd visited everyone who was home and now it was time for her one adventure of the day. She wanted to go out. She sat outside the door meowing at me, getting angrier by the minute. I kept telling her, 'Just a minute. Hold on.' But she was tired of waiting.

When I finally surfaced from the last bit of grading, I looked around. I couldn't find her. I knocked on the other teachers' doors,

 33

but none of them had seen her. I quickly became quite frantic. The door to the stairwell was closed; she couldn't have gone down there. I went back to my apartment to see if she was hiding, determined to punish me for my lack of attention. But she wasn't there either.

Finally, in desperation, I took the elevator downstairs to alert the guards that my cat was missing. They laughed, and nodded wildly as if I was making a joke. They knew where she was. They pointed at the doors. I rushed outside to find her playing in the cool grass, just as she normally did. She blinked happily, as if she couldn't understand all the bother as I hurried to pick her up, relieved to finally find her.

Apparently, about an hour before, she'd decided that if she went and stood where I did, the elevator would open for her too. Of course, since I lived in a busy building and someone was always going up or down, it did. It took her right down to the downstairs lobby, and the doors outside. She'd strutted past the security desk and confidently stood in front of the lobby doors, waiting for the guards to open one for her. They had. And out she went.

She'd managed to get on the elevator, take it to the right floor and calmly exit it with the aplomb of a determined feline. Getting the guards to open the doors for her in itself was quite a feat. (I've only seen them run to open the doors for the university president. Lesser officials and instructors like myself have to do it on their own. For Sasha, however, they opened the doors.) She had become the elevator cat.

After that I had to be careful about letting her wander the hallway. Her 'visiting' would turn into unexpected outings. This rescued cat was resourceful and smart, and a very good friend for many years.

By Sharman Horwood, a Canadian writer living and working in Seoul, South Korea

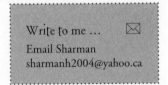

Write to me ...

Email Sharman
sharmanh2004@yahoo.ca

4

Rescued animals are heroes

We saved each other

My story is about Echo, a little Australian shepherd who was born deaf and blind.

Echo was going to be shot, but when I saw her sitting in the middle of the driveway, screaming at the top of her lungs for her mama, I knew she was a fighter. We took Echo home with us.

I had just been told I was going to be in a wheelchair for the rest of my life, and I was depressed. Echo became my saviour. I watched her as she learned to use her front feet to feel where things were, and her nose to find her food dishes. She learned to go down the stairs in one day using her front paws and a harness. She can find her way from the back of our 2.5 acre property to the front door in less than five minutes. As I watched her learn how to do these everyday things, I thought, 'If she can handle being blind and deaf, I can handle this wheelchair.'

Thanks to my wonderful Echo, I not only learned how to deal with the wheelchair, I am no longer in it! Her courage and tenacity gave me the will to get up and walk, and to start a rescue centre for animals with disabilities.

Echo is the best and most cherished girl in the world. She loves Christmas and can open anything you put in front of her. She loves to play with her dad (me), is very quick and is also quite sneaky

 35

– she can get out any door without being seen, to go on merry adventures.

Echo is the smartest, most confident dog I have ever seen. She is worth everything to us and she will be my saviour forever.

By Mickey Scurio, Buffalo, Wyoming, United States of America

Write to me ...

Mickey Scurio
PO Box 1119
Buffalo, WY 82834
USA
email: babbydoll@hughes.net

Wonderful Gypsy

Gypsy is a mongrel who started life as a stray and was rescued by the RSPCA. She was then selected by Hearing Dogs for Deaf People, and at the age of one year she was chosen as my hearing dog. I have had her for three years now. I am profoundly deaf, but with her as my 'ears' I become a hearing person. She is my best friend – a wonderful and loyal companion.

I have another best friend, my 14-year-old dog Charlie. A few years ago he started having fits and breathing attacks, and losing his sight and hearing. To my amazement, Gypsy mothers Charlie and alerts me when he is in distress. For example, Charlie is terrified of thunderstorms, and one afternoon when I was reading in the living room Gypsy alerted me and led me to the French doors. I saw that there was a hailstorm occurring, with thunder. Then she led me to Charlie's basket, where he was cowering and very frightened, and so I was able to comfort him.

It doesn't stop there either – because of his poor eyesight she also leads him on our walks and will fetch him on command if he strays and is unable to find us. A couple of years ago, when I was walking both dogs and throwing balls for them to chase, Charlie went in one direction and Gypsy in another. Gypsy was halfway towards her ball when she stopped and ran back to Charlie, whom I hadn't seen running in the other direction. Charlie had ruptured a ligament in his knee joint and was in agony. Gypsy started licking him as I comforted him, and I managed to get them both back home. She accompanied me in the ambulance to the animal hospital, which gave me great comfort. Thankfully, he is now fully recovered.

Recently Gypsy came to Charlie's rescue again. One morning at about 3 am when my husband and I were fast asleep, Gypsy woke me up. She kept pushing me with her paws until I finally asked, 'What is it?' She shot over to the closed door, so I got up and opened the door and followed her to the landing. There I found Charlie under the computer table. He had somehow become entangled in the wires under the table and a cord was wound round his neck. He was choking as he struggled to free himself. I untangled him, and was very grateful to Gypsy for alerting me to his distress.

Gypsy has transformed my life in so many ways. She has opened my eyes to the outside world by making me notice wildlife, she alerts me to danger, and she breaks down communication barriers for me. I could go on forever, because Gypsy is a very special dog to me!

By Janet Durbridge,
Milton Keyes,
Buckinghamshire, England

Find out more:
www.hearing-dogs.org.uk

Write to me ... ✉

Mrs Janet Durbridge
c/o Hearing Dogs for Deaf People
The Grange, Wycombe Road
Saunderton, Princes Risborough
Buckinghamshire
HP27 9NS
United Kingdom

. 37

My incredible Sasha

photo p79

In December 2004 I became a foster mum for a local cat welfare group. My first charge was a tiny four-week-old grey kitten with black whiskers and a minute black nose. Sasha had been found under a bush in a reserve – starving, scared and injured. Her right back leg was missing a paw, leaving a stump with a bony protrusion which she pushed forward to line up with her front paws. My vet was certain that someone had deliberately removed the paw and then simply discarded her. Sadly, it meant her right back leg would have to be removed.

Sasha was too young for the operation and we had to wait another month. I basked in the delight of caring for Sasha. She developed a unique way of getting around – on her bottom! She looked like a little gothic creature, all hunched up and wearing a grumpy expression which reflected her disdain for what life had dealt her at such a young age. She was a determined little soul.

Operation day arrived. We brought her home and kept her in a holding cage to prevent too much movement. That night Sasha gave me a new respect for and insight into animals. She was so angry – angry at the pain, at us, and at whoever had done this to her. She rocked from side to side in her cage, screaming. It was horrendous. I stayed up with her all night, and I vowed I would give her the life she deserved and so much more. But I had to consult my two other furry children, ex-SPCA cats Tobie and Puurdie, on this matter and I knew it would be no easy task.

I started taking Sasha downstairs to get her used to her new surroundings. Tobie was wary: he seemed to be wondering if she actually *was* a feline! Sasha does not have the sleek physique of a cat. She hops rather than walks and, out of habit, pushes her remaining back leg forward in line with her front paws. Puurdie forgot her very dignified self and simply turned scary. Being my constant companion and having me firmly under her paw, she was insanely jealous. Drama all round! Out of pure desperation the three of us went behind closed doors and had a heart-to-heart about why Sasha should stay.

I let Sasha out of her cage for the first time and we never looked back. Sasha wasn't interested in her surroundings, only the resident cats. She knew that her priority was to befriend Tobie and Puurdie. As always, she was determined to fit in. She learnt every game and eased effortlessly into our routine. Now Big Tobie has become protective of her, and as for Sasha and Princess Puurdie they are inseparable!

Sasha continues to amaze us. I kept her indoors for a long time but I should never have doubted her determination. On her first day out, she scaled our 1.7 metre wooden fence and proceeded to hop along a five centimetre width of wood, 'tightrope' style. I laughed out loud, clapped my hands and cried that day. On another occasion, Sasha managed to climb down a 2.8 metre wall at the side of our house from an upstairs balcony!

She is slowly regaining her trust in people. Every night she scrambles onto the couch, lying at my side to get her belly rubbed. Her favourite thing in life is the raw beef she gets at suppertime.

A few months after her operation, Sasha developed a perfect diamond of white fur in the centre of her chest. I refer to it as Sasha's medal of honour.

You may think I'm obsessed with her. You're right – and I'll tell you why. I have suffered from manic depression for 11 years now. Before Sasha came to me I had gone through two hellish years: never leaving the house, never leaving my bed, trying endless medications, undergoing ECT (electroconvulsive therapy) and attempting suicide.

When Sasha came into my nightmarish existence she brought her tremendous spirit and strength, which turned out to be contagious. Without realising it, I began to pick up the pieces of my life. No matter how rotten I felt I knew I had to get out of bed and take care of her. Sasha gave me purpose in an otherwise bleak situation. She is not overly affectionate, but even on a bad day she is at my side.

Sasha is my constant in life. She does not go to my husband or anyone else, only me. Together we are survivors. Animals have incredible healing powers and I have proof of this in my three-legged bundle of fur. On bad days, Sasha will dance around me as if she's saying, *Hey, I've only got three legs, you've got a messed up head, so what? Let's play a game and I'll make you laugh!* Her remedy never fails – she is my miracle drug. In life there are some things you just don't question – I rescued Sasha, and she rescued me right back.

By Suzanne Post, Auckland, New Zealand

Boots – such a wonderful dog

We called him Boots because of the four white paws that he wears with his white chest and rich jet-black coat. His mom and dad were working cattle dogs, and their 12 Australian shepherd pups urgently needed a home before the folks who owned them destroyed those not lucky enough to find a new family. Of course, we fell in love at first sight and Boots became part of our family.

We run a ranch in the rugged forested mountains of British Columbia where we raise both cattle and horses. Here, a good stock dog is invaluable and Boots has proven to us that even an untrained one can do wondrous things.

The fall of 2003 saw British Columbia riddled with huge forest fires due to the unusually hot and dry drought conditions we had experienced that summer. On July 31, 2003 one of those forest fires became a raging wildfire above our ranch, rapidly rolling towards us and consuming everything in its path.

As I loaded horses for emergency evacuation with the help of numerous friends and neighbours, my husband Bob went up on the mountain behind our ranch to bring down the 50 head of cattle and their calves that were summer-ranging there. The mountain would become a trap when the fire arrived, as there was only one way off and we knew the fire would quickly block that exit.

Ever mindful of his animals' safety, Bob refused to take a dog or a horse up the mountain to help him bring the cattle down, so he did it on foot. His run down the mountain with all but 17 of the 83 head of cattle is a story of its own, but he did it in record time – and just in time too.

As the cattle came into our barnyard they were very agitated. By now there was smoke from the fire everywhere and many of the cattle had become separated from their calves during the all-out run to the corrals. The mountain directly across the river from us (a distance of less than a mile) was a boiling sea of flame that created its own defining sounds as the trees succumbed to the flames. The noise from the stock trailers as the cattle were forced into them added to the din, creating even more panic.

One calf broke away from the group and doubled back towards the mountain. Nature has given calves the instinct to return to the last place they nursed from their mom when they cannot find her. Unfortunately, the last place this calf nursed was now a rolling sea of 100 foot flames where pine trees exploded like Roman candles as wildfire consumed them.

We tried to corner the frightened calf and turn him back, but he was too determined to return to where he believed his mother was.

41

He kept ducking past us and heading further from the barnyard and closer to the fire.

Having brought this little guy safely off the mountain Bob was determined not to see him run back up into the fire, so he turned to the closest help he could find – Boots. Now, being a young dog, Boots had received very little stock training up to this point in his life. However, when you're desperate for help, even an overeager untrained Australian shepherd might make a difference.

So Bob let Boots out of the truck and sent him after the mountain-bound calf, who was by now a good ten acres from the barnyard and distancing himself further from it with every second that passed. I don't know what Bob said to the dog, but he pointed Boots at that calf and the dog was off like a bullet.

A single calf in an unfenced area is extremely hard for one dog to move towards a given point, if that calf is determined to go in another direction. They will continually double back, run madly in the wrong direction and, in desperation, lose all fear of the dog and run over it to get to where they want to go. This particular calf tried it all, but our wonderful Boots never wavered. He kept that baby heading back to the barnyard – all at top speed and completely on his own.

I cried when I saw Boots hustling that calf up to the few remaining cows we still had to load. He was totally exhausted, his tongue was hanging out and he was breathing so hard I thought he would pass out, but he was smiling. That 'I'm such a wonderful dog' smile that animal lovers the world over know so well.

And he *was* a wonderful dog. He had done something I never would have thought possible. Boots somehow knew that we wanted that calf back in the barnyard as quickly as possible. He used his intelligence and inherited ability to not only understand the situation but also to recognise the problem and how to solve it. He out-thought a desperate calf and proved he is 'smarter than Jack'.

Yes, we were able to get all of the animals in the barnyard safely away before the flames claimed the ranch. We have rebuilt and Boots is still an important part of our family. He still wears his 'I'm such a wonderful dog' smile, because he knows he truly is.

By Jill Hayward, Louis Creek,
British Columbia, Canada

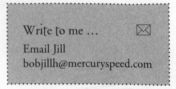
Write to me …

Email Jill
bobjillh@mercuryspeed.com

Cherry makes an arrest

Cherry was a funny little dog, being a Rottweiler/Staffy cross – a strange combination. She looked like a Staffy with a Rottweiler's head. She was difficult to home and had been at the kennels for nearly a year. The vet was worried that she was being affected by staying in the kennels too long and was considering putting her to sleep. Luckily, a young man who was looking for a companion adopted her. They seemed to bond very well and we were happy with the adoption.

I was carrying out the follow-up inspection to see how Cherry had settled in. She seemed happy with her new life and I asked her new owner how she was getting on. He said, 'She not only saved my life but made an arrest as well.'

The story is as follows. One night, Cherry's owner was awoken by a burglar entering through his bedroom window. Cherry was sleeping on his bed and immediately leapt into action. The burglar had one leg through the window, and Cherry grabbed hold of it

.43

and wouldn't let go. The burglar was screaming, but Cherry just bit down harder with the combined strength of a Rottie and a Staffy. She held on until the police arrived and took away the burglar via the local hospital.

As most burglars in South Africa are armed, Cherry not only stopped a burglary, she protected her owner by holding on until the police arrived. A courageous girl who was 'smarter than Jack'.

By Steve Maxworthy,
Greek Animal Welfare Fund,
London, England

Write to me …

Email Steve
stevemaxworthy@yahoo.co.uk

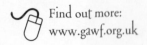

Find out more:
www.gawf.org.uk

Delta's new life

photo
p79

When Hurricane Katrina hit, there were many animals in need of assistance. I work for the Nebraska Humane Society, and I knew we would be helping in every way we possibly could. First, we sent staff down to Mississippi to assist in temporary animal shelters that were set up to help the major influx of animals who had lost their families. Later, I found out we would be sending down a caravan of five conversion vans (vans with the rear area converted to a living space) to bring home cats and dogs. I wanted to be part of that caravan, and my wish came true!

The drive took about 24 hours. When we finally arrived, we were amazed at how well the Humane Society of the United States (HSUS) had organised and cared for these hundreds of animals in the Hattiesburg, Mississippi fairgrounds.

Our first order of business was to assess the temperament and health of the dogs the HSUS had selected for us to take home. All the dogs were in better shape than I had imagined. However, I am a devout lover of golden retrievers, and I was shocked when I saw the state of a small golden retriever cross selected for us to take home. She had little hair on her face and head and no hair on her tail or back legs, and was about 15 pounds underweight. The notes on her records said she wouldn't eat unless someone sat with her. When I touched her food bowl, she froze – the classic action of a dog who is probably food-aggressive.

The trip home with the 43 dogs and 40-odd cats was interesting. The reception we got when we pulled in to the shelter melted my heart. All the staff and many volunteers were there cheering us on, which was just what we needed.

All the dogs would need medical attention, and we were to hold them for 30 days awaiting their owners. Of course I loved them all, but I was particularly worried about the golden. I checked on her daily. She had severe heartworm disease and severe skin allergies. She was assigned to me for walks and socialisation, and I decided to foster her. At the suggestion of a friend who was a shelter volunteer I named her Delta.

As it turned out, she was not even remotely food-aggressive. She sure had other problems, though! The heartworm treatment left her tired and she panted all the time. She had pellets under her skin, which means she must have been shot at some time in her life. Having had several litters of puppies, she was in desperate need of being spayed. A blood test listed three pages of food, plants and other things she was allergic to. She will be on medication and a special diet for the rest of her life and will battle these allergies forever.

She needed emotional help as well: she had been beaten. She wasn't scared of my hand, but if I had something in it, like a pen, she

45

dropped to the floor, urinated and flinched, waiting for her beating. What was I going to do with this dog? I had my own pets to worry about!

Delta's owner did not claim her, so I decided to adopt her – I just loved her! Then, everything in my personal life changed. I had to move out of my home, and I did the hardest thing I have ever had to do: I left all my pets except Delta and two of my cats. I left them in capable hands, yet I missed them so much I ached – and still do. Without Delta, this transition would have been much more difficult. I take her everywhere with me. She helps me in my obedience classes, helps to temperament-test dogs, helps train the inmates in our prison programme and helps to socialise dogs who need a playmate. The list of people and animals she has helped just keeps getting longer.

Delta looks like a golden now, with a fully furred tail, legs and head. She has gained almost 15 pounds, and she shows absolutely no signs of aggression. She does not flinch or think she is going to be beaten any more, which makes me very happy. She may not be the perfect dog, but she is the perfect dog for me. She came all the way from a hurricane to help me through the most difficult time in my life. They say everything happens for a reason. I believe that now. In the end, Delta has saved me more than I saved her.

By Nikki Harris, Omaha,
Nebraska, United States of America

Write to me …

Email Nikki
nlharris2000@yahoo.com

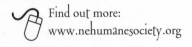

Find out more:
www.nehumanesociety.org

Photo provided by Bridget Egan

Ben makes sure all is well

Ben saves the day

We have two Cats Protection 'rescue' cats, Ben and Tiny. One very cold winter's afternoon as I sat watching a film on TV, Ben came in and started clawing at the back of my chair. Thinking he was just being naughty, I told him off. He went away, then a minute later he was back and started again, clawing even harder this time.

Eventually I stood up to see what he wanted, grumbling that I was missing my film. He led me into the kitchen and stood there, looking up. Water was dripping through the light fitting onto the floor. One of the taps in the bathroom (which was directly over the kitchen) had sprung a leak, and water was going everywhere.

I called my husband and we went up to deal with it. Ben looked at us as if to say, *I told you something was wrong!* Then, his job done, he climbed into his bed and promptly went to sleep. Needless to say, he got extra-special cuddles that evening.

By Bridget Egan, Broadstairs, Kent, England

Write to me ... ✉
Email Bridget
egans@bushinternet.com

 Find out more:
www.cats.org.uk

Fan-taz-tic hearing dog Taz

photo
p80

My best friend Taz was handed over as a six-month-old pup to a dogs' home in Cardiff, as his original family felt they could no longer give him the time and attention he needed. He has a lovely temperament and, two weeks later, Hearing Dogs for Deaf People picked him up. He completed his sound-work training, and it was at the end of November 1999 that I met Taz for the first time.

We had five days working together, getting to know each other and forming a bond. At the end of the week, I was able to bring him home. The deaf children at St John's Unit in Kenilworth, where I work, loved him and gave him the sign name of Taz (whirlwind). He has also helped two teachers to overcome their fear of dogs.

Like most hearing dogs, Taz has been trained to alert me to the doorbell, fax, cooker timer, alarm clock and smoke alarm. He has taken it upon himself to alert me to the arrival of my husband Mike's motorbike! We also use Taz to call each other if one of us is upstairs. Nowadays, when I am cooking dinner Taz seems to know when it is ready and fetches Mike from the study room upstairs without me having to ask him to.

Taz has proved what an exceptional dog he is by alerting me to a potential fire and a room full of smoke when our water boiler broke down.

On another occasion, a group of us went walking up Snowdon (a mountain in Wales). We somehow got separated into two groups as we climbed nearer to the summit, with me and Mike in the faster group. The mist came down and we could no longer see the slower group, who were not too far behind us. My sister-in-law Katie, who was in the slower group, called Taz. Off he went to join them. Katie then told him to call me, so he came back to our group and alerted me to the situation.

Leaving the faster group waiting, Mike and I went back to the others to find out what was up. It turned out that one of the men had pulled a muscle in his leg and needed assistance to reach the cafe at the top of the summit. If Taz had not alerted us, we would have carried on to the cafe without realising what had happened to the slower group and wondered what had befallen them.

More recently, I fell down the stairs and landed on my knees on the quarry-tiled floor in the hall, yelling out in pain. Mike was sitting in the lounge watching TV, when Taz heard me yelling and frantically alerted Mike, leading him to find me in lots of pain on the floor.

Taz has his own unique personality that says *Look, I am here!* wherever he goes. To sum it all up, Taz is a 'fan-Taz-tic' hearing dog to have and I would be lost without him!

By Mags Adams-Aston,
Warwickshire, England

Write to me ...

Email Mags
maxi1750@hotmail.com

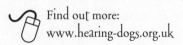
Find out more:
www.hearing-dogs.org.uk

Inseparable friends

photo
p80

For most horses, keeping them on their own is not the kindest thing to do, as they are herd animals. One horse I owned many years ago, a cremello Quarter cross gelding called Tyson, definitely needed companionship. He paced the fences like a condemned man, neighing constantly. He quickly lost condition, not only from the continual frenetic movement but also because he refused to settle and eat more than a few mouthfuls at a time.

My husband and I couldn't afford another horse; we had just bought a small acreage and were in the process of renovating the farm cottage. Luckily, a short time later we were offered a mare at the right price. Connie Red was a five-year-old chestnut ex-racehorse. Tyson fell in love with her instantly and, much to her (sometimes obvious) annoyance, didn't let her out of his sight.

On Ash Wednesday – February 16, 1983 – Australia suffered one of its worst bush fires. One of the areas worst hit was the south-east of South Australia, where we live. I was running the farm by myself that day, as my husband Martin had gone to work. At the time, I had a 13-week-old daughter, a four-year-old son, and another son on crutches recovering from a bone tumour operation.

A wind change caused the fire to divert towards our property, giving us no warning and no time to prepare. There wasn't time to move the horses to a safer place, or even to find our little dog Candy (thankfully, she survived). I barely got our children to the safety of the town's football oval, before the thick ash blocked out the sun and the fire roared through like a raging monster.

I prayed that my horses would be all right. I had let them out of their day yard and I hoped they would both be spared, somehow.

Martin finally got through the police roadblock and, not knowing where we were, headed towards our farm. When we were finally reunited, he told me what had happened. When he got to the farm there were spot fires everywhere. Trees were still ablaze and all the sheds and fences were gone. His first concern was to stop our little cottage from going up in smoke. A corner was already alight, but luckily a trough still contained water and he was able to douse the flames by bucket.

As he did so, he noticed a strange sight: the horses. Although appearing unhurt, they were very agitated. The strange thing was the way they were moving. Then he saw a pattern emerging. Connie, living up to her fractious thoroughbred nature, was trying to gallop away and, because all the fences were burnt, she could have easily done so, except for one thing – Tyson was heading her off.

He was effectively rounding her up, keeping her safely on the one small area of unburnt grass in what was left of the paddock. He must have been doing this the whole time the fire front had been passing through.

It was an amazing sight, Martin told me. 'Over and over again Connie would make a dash, but Tyson was quicker, sliding to a halt directly in front of her. Then he'd bar her with his chest and, by repeatedly tossing his head, seemed to be telling her to stay where she was. He kept her there by running round and round, encircling her.'

We have no doubt that Tyson saved Connie's life, as all our other livestock perished that day. Both horses went on to live well into their twenties. They were never separated, and even in death they went together.

By Myra Taankink, Tarpeena,
South Australia

Write to me ... ✉
Myra Taankink
c/o Post Office
Tarpeena, SA 5277
Australia

Duck seeks help for her children

July 13, 2001, CANADA – A civilian member of the Vancouver, British Columbia police has a new take on the term 'birdbrain' after a duck pestered him until he helped rescue her eight ducklings trapped in a storm sewer.

Ray Peterson was walking directly under the Granville Bridge when the duck grabbed him by the pant leg. Then she waddled around him, quacking.

'I thought she was a bit goofy, so I shoved her away,' Mr Peterson said.

But the duck, who looked like a mallard, wouldn't give up. Making sure she still had Mr Peterson's eye, she waddled up the road about 20 metres and lay on a storm sewer grate. Mr Peterson watched and thought nothing of it. 'But when I started walking again, she did the same thing. She ran around me and grabbed me again.'

So when the duck waddled off to the sewer grate a second time, Mr Peterson followed.

'I went up to where the duck was lying and saw eight little babies in the water below. They had fallen down between the grates.'

Mr Peterson phoned police sergeant Randy Kellens, who brought in two constables. 'When they came down the duck ran around them as well, quacking,' Mr Peterson said. 'Then she lay down on the grate.'

While Sgt Kellens looked into the grate, the duck sat on the kerb and watched. The two constables marshalled a tow truck that lifted the grate out, allowing the ducklings to be picked up one by one with a vegetable strainer.

'While we were doing this, the mother duck just lay there and watched,' Mr Peterson said.

Once they were safe, however, she marched down to False Creek, where they all jumped in.

From 'The Canadian Press'

Scarlett: cat of the century

It was a story that touched the hearts of people throughout the world. In early 1996 a mother cat pulled her five kittens to safety from a blazing abandoned building in Brooklyn, USA, badly scorching herself. One kitten, weakened by smoke inhalation, died of a virus. The four remaining four-week-old kittens recuperated with her at an animal clinic.

With her eyes blistered shut, her paws burned and her coat singed, the cat (nicknamed Scarlett) darted into the flames and pulled out her kittens, one by one. Once all the kittens had been rescued, their mother conducted a head count, touching each kitten with her nose to make sure they were all there.

Firefighter David Giannelli, a 17-year veteran with Ladder Company 175, told reporters, 'What she did was she ran in and out of that building five times, got them all out and then started moving them one by one across the street.' David found the feline family outside the building and took them to an animal shelter, where the mother and babies received treatment. His colleagues coined a nickname for firefighter David: 'the animal guy'. 'Everyone here knows that anything I can do for an animal I'll do,' David said.

Three months after her heroic feat, Scarlett and her four surviving babies were not only well, but were adopted in a blaze of publicity. After reading hundreds of letters from people who wanted to adopt the cats, a committee at North Shore Animal League picked three families.

Two kittens, Oreo and Smokey, went to Debbie Palmarozzo of Miller Place, Long Island. 'I might change Smokey's name to Cinders,' said Debbie. The two other kittens, Samsara and Panuki – who have been inseparable – are with Corinne and Ginette Vercillo of Port Washington, Long Island.

As for Scarlett, judging by all the cat hair on her new owner, Karen, there was some heavy bonding going on. 'I expected to see a scrawny hairless cat and she was gorgeous,' said Karen. Named for her burned-red flesh, Scarlett is certainly more like the feisty heroine of *Gone with the Wind*. Karen's letter caught the committee's eye because she told of losing her own cat seven years ago shortly after she herself was hurt in a car accident. 'The physical and emotional pain I suffered made me more compassionate, and I vowed if ever allowed another cat in my home it would be one with special needs,' Karen wrote.

Scarlett is special, all right. 'We spoiled her rotten,' said Dr Bonnie Brown of North Shore Animal League. 'Scarlett is used to being queen of North Shore Animal League.'

Scarlett even has a website devoted to her, featuring a poem entitled *Why is Everybody So Surprised that I Saved My Furry Five?* She is also the subject of a book, *Scarlett Saves Her Family*.

Undoubtedly, Scarlett and her children live in the lap of luxury. 'My husband's building a cat condo ten feet tall,' said one proud new owner. 'I went out and bought everything that wasn't tied down in the pet store,' said another.

Maybe, just maybe, this will be the end of Scarlett fever.

From Moggies Website at www.moggies.co.uk

5

Rescued animals spot a good thing

Birds definitely have brains

My neighbour's ten-year-old son came to our door one Saturday morning to say that a blackbird was hanging by its leg from a branch of our viburnum tree. We found that the leg was tied to the branch by a length of blue cotton, evidently being taken to the nest for building purposes or repairs.

In his struggle to free himself he had abraded all the feathers on his back from neck to tail, and the flesh was raw and bleeding.

On further inspection we found that the left leg was so strained that the claw would not function and grip things properly. So, after treating him for shock, bathing his wounds and massaging his left hip and leg, my husband and the lad went down the garden to the compost heap and dug up some worms for the bird. Because birds lose one quarter of their weight during the night, they must eat an early breakfast. This poor soul had eaten nothing that morning, and may not even have eaten the night before.

He ate the worms with gusto but was still quiet and in need of rest, so every 20 minutes or so we attended to him. We gave him water, worms or whatever he needed and nestled him in a softly lined box in the dark to recover.

55

Then we saw that he was collecting the worms in his beak, not eating them, and realised that he wanted to feed his young in the nest. We inspected him again and found that the left leg was now much better and the claw was beginning to grip as it should, so we released him among some bushes below his tree and left him to attend to his business.

A while later we were in the lounge, when we saw the blackbird's mate creeping along a branch that extended across the window. She kept turning her head from side to side as if to get a good look at us. We had not seen much of her before and she certainly had never been such a nosy bird, so we laughingly suggested that the blackbird must have gone back to the nest and told his mate about the folk who nursed him, and she became curious to see us. Well, who knows, maybe that's why she came to the window!

However, the best part was still to come. My husband Stan went out to the garden shed the next morning and the bird flew onto the roof. When Stan emerged from the shed, the bird flew round his head three times and then flew back to its nest. We took that to be a salute of 'thank you'!

And people say birds have no brains. They couldn't be more wrong.

By Gwen Keene, Upper Hutt, New Zealand

Grateful Biskit

Our cat Biskit has been with us for a couple of years now. He was a very beaten-up stray who showed up on our doorstep on and off for eight months, always hungry and usually bashed up from a fight. I planned to get him neutered, but thought that he would remain an occasional guest. At that point we wanted to get a dog and, as we already had two cats in our small home, we didn't have room for another permanent cat as well.

One day, Biskit showed up barely able to walk. It took me three weeks to catch him so that I could get him looked at. He obviously did not have an owner – or not one that was prepared to look after him properly. Anyway, after keeping him confined in the house so that I could give him his antibiotics, I realised the dog would have to wait. Biskit needed us more.

Biskit was scared of so many things. I don't know what had happened to him but it can't have been good. Absolutely anywhere I went in the house, he went too. He became my shadow. I think this was his way of showing his gratitude to me for getting his wounds cleaned and his sore foot looked after. He doesn't like being outside any more; he just wants to live a comfortable life indoors.

The funny thing is that you never have to tell him anything twice. Once you've shown him what is expected of him, he does the right thing from then on. All three cats know they are not allowed on our bed unless they lie on the special kitty blanket, but the other two are constantly breaking that rule. Not Biskit, though – I think he is scared of disappointing us. 'Biskit, on the kitty blanket,' we say, and up he gets. When we come home and check on him, he is always on the kitty blanket.

One day we came home and checked on him, and I couldn't believe my eyes. We hadn't made the bed, and there was only the tiniest piece of the kitty blanket left on top of it, right at the edge. And there was Biskit, lying on top of that little piece, with not a bit of his fur touching our bed. His legs were dangling over the side and he was struggling to keep from sliding off. He looked so funny but, at the same time, so sweet, because he always tries so hard to be a good boy. If you could see our Biskit's big fat tummy, you would know that it was not an easy task for him to perform!

57

I think rescued animals are different because, having known hardship, they give you back twice the love, to thank you for loving them and keeping them safe. They are so grateful and want nothing more than to please you. We are glad that Biskit chose our doorstep.

By Karen Mol, Perth,
Western Australia

Write to me … ✉
Karen Mol
7d Chailey Place
Balga, Perth, WA 6061
Australia
email: misslestat@hotmail.com

Smokey: retired military feral

At first glance, Smokey appears to be the dumbest of our four cats. While the two kittens wrestle and play and Nocturne keeps a careful watch over the household, Smokey spends his days lolling on a couch, gazing with rapt fascination at the ceiling. He lavishes affection on any and all guests, as undiscriminating as a dog, and his only fear is an empty food bowl.

But Smokey wasn't always a spoiled house pet. When I first saw him in May 2002, he was a gaunt shadow creeping around the premises of the Royal Canadian Air Cadets gliding school, where I was an administration officer. When he couldn't catch bunnies or seagulls, he'd launch nocturnal raids on our trash cans. The security operations personnel quickly learned not to leave a pizza box unattended outside.

The chief of security was a tough-talking captain with a soft spot for animals. It wasn't long before a dish of cat food appeared outside the operations centre door. Soon the feline began making regular appearances in the smoking pit, where he would rub against the captain and maybe get a bite to eat out of a military box lunch. Because of his new hangout and his grey coat, the cat was quickly named Smokey. Animals were forbidden inside the barracks but Smokey made himself at home outside, and soon he was the unofficial mascot of the gliding school.

Unfortunately, there were other individuals much less impressed by the 'wild animal' who had come to call the gliding school home. In August, the captain got orders that he was no longer allowed to feed Smokey – they didn't want to encourage 'wildlife' to hang around the barracks. While Smokey was well loved, nobody seemed to have a permanent home to offer. When the 'no feeding' policy came into effect, we needed to find Smokey a new place to live right away.

I phoned my partner with four fateful words: 'Can we have Smokey?' The question was not without a certain degree of risk. We lived in a high-rise – a very different environment from the forest around the barracks. For all we knew, Smokey had never been indoors. Would he torment Nocturne, our other cat? Would he learn to use a litter box? Would he adapt to life in an apartment?

The captain gave me a leave pass to take Smokey to our apartment. Putting Smokey in a carrier was easy – we simply waited for him to show up at the operations centre for dinner, then picked him up and dropped him in. He was terrified, screaming and thrashing for the hour-long drive to my place. Once the carrier was open, he stepped out tentatively, staring at the walls, the ceiling, the carpet, as though he'd found himself on another planet. He panicked, tried to jump out of the window and collided with the glass; cringing, he crouched down under the end table. From there, Smokey made careful forays to explore his new environment.

59

We had some heartbreaking moments, such as the morning when Smokey cried in front of the garbage pail, hoping we'd let him lick bacon grease and eggshells. His cat food went untouched; he couldn't believe it was for him, and so he begged for trash. It took much coaxing and petting to show him that it was okay to eat the cat food. Similarly, he cried for permission to sit on the couch. Always soft, never damp, designed solely for luxury, the couch was a marvel to the cat who'd sheltered from snow and rain under a trailer.

Smokey adapted immediately to the litter box. However, he wasn't familiar with television: the moving images fascinated him, and he began circling round the back of the TV, hoping to come up behind the 'animals' and pounce on them. Smokey was immediately enamoured with Nocturne, but it took her several weeks to learn to tolerate him. The vet became Smokey's best friend with the gift of a few kibbles.

We knew Smokey had found his permanent home on the day we attempted to take him outside for a walk on a leash and harness. We thought he might miss the outdoors. Instead, Smokey threw himself on the ground and screamed until we brought him back inside. He had found a home that was always warm, always dry, always contained food – he wanted nothing to do with outside, where he had survived through rain, snow, intense heat and hunger.

Smokey's a goofball. Smokey's a slug. But when I see Smokey sprawled on the couch, I see a cat revelling in the fact that he's got the only thing he ever wanted – a home. When you've got a belly full of food, a roof over your head, a soft couch under your butt and a family who loves you, what more do you really need? Sometimes when I'm fussing because I can't afford a book or CD without breaking my budget, I look over at Smokey, squinting with pleasure at simply having one more day to enjoy life's bounty ... and I remember what's really important.

And sometimes I wonder if Smokey's really our dumbest cat. It's hard to give that label to a cat who's succeeded in getting everything he ever wanted.

By Mary Pletsch, Halifax,
Nova Scotia, Canada

Write to me ... ✉
Email Mary
marypletsch@hotmail.com

The courteous bee

One day, after a night of heavy rain, I went to get our two goats from their stall to take them across to the paddock. The goats' stall had guttering along the front and I noticed it was full of water. Floating in the water was a bumblebee – probably a queen who had woken from hibernation and been searching for somewhere to start her colony when she was beaten down by the rain, washed down into the guttering and drowned.

I decided to play lifeguard and lifted her out on my finger. No signs of life. I took her indoors, tore off a length of paper towel and slid her onto it. As the paper became wet, I moved her across it until there were no more drops of water, but still she showed no signs of reviving.

My husband had laid the breakfast table, so I dipped my finger in the honey pot and held it out to the bee. Immediately, her tongue unfurled and dipped into the honey. After a hearty satisfying breakfast, she started grooming herself. Soon her velvet suit was fluffy and shiny. Her toilette completed, she started to walk across the table. If she fell off the edge, one of our cats or dogs might have come to investigate, so I placed a tumbler over her and went back to the now impatient goats.

61

When I returned, my husband reported that the bee had been exploring her invisible prison, becoming exasperated every time she met the glass. I removed the tumbler and held my finger out in front of her. Either attracted by the heat or recognising that this was her next method of travel, she climbed straight on. I took her out the front door and stood on the step with my husband, my hand held out in the breeze.

After some experimental stretching of her wings, she rose into the air and took off. Across the garden, across the road and over the bush, until she was a mere speck in the distance. Suddenly, she did a U-turn and headed back along the same route. As she came closer I realised she was heading towards my face, and felt my neck muscles tighten as I prepared to duck. But, inches from my nose, she turned sharply to the right and did a tight circle round my head. Then, with a final buzz, she was off along the same route for the third time, and this time she did not return.

As we turned to go inside, my husband remarked, 'What a polite bee. She came all the way back to say thank you.'

By Fay Gibbens, Greymouth,
New Zealand

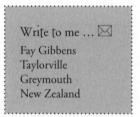

Write to me ... ✉

Fay Gibbens
Taylorville
Greymouth
New Zealand

Lulu the smiling dog

When I was a child my parents allowed us to have many different pets, but when it came to dogs they chose to have Dobermanns. As an adult, I moved from mainland USA to Hawaii. One day I heard a radio advertisement for Doby/ridgeback puppies, and decided to go and see them.

There were only two puppies left and they were in bad shape. The puppies' owners fished for a living and fed the dogs only fish guts. Also, they let their very young kids play with them, which meant lots of rough handling. The puppies cowered and hid when I looked for them. When I eventually got them out from their hiding place, they were not like normal puppies. They seemed dissociated from their surroundings, and had no fun puppy playfulness about them. I felt sorry for them and immediately took both puppies.

My friend helped me get them home. When we got there, they hid in the tall pasture grass in the adjacent property. It took two hours to find them. When we finally brought them down to the house, they hid under it, terrified. We showered them with love and affection. We called these times 'love sessions', and initially the puppies hated them because they couldn't stand such close contact with humans.

But, of course, love eventually won out and they grew up to be wonderful dogs. I named them Lulu and Nika. I think as a result of their early puppyhood, Lulu had a habit of 'smiling'. The vet told me it was an act of submission, but I found she also did it when she received a treat or met someone new. Her smile was so large, and her whole body wagged so much with joy, that she became famous at all the gas stations and other outdoor places I frequented. If I didn't have Lulu in the back of my pickup, people would ask, 'Where is Lulu today?'

She also had a habit of bringing people 'presents'. It was usually whatever she found lying closest to her. One time a lady asked me if I'd taught her to pick up trash, because she had picked up a wrapper and handed it to a stranger who was walking by. When I came home she would pick something up – a leaf or anything – and, with that huge smile and joyful wagging body, bring it to me as a gift.

When I moved to the other side of the island, the girls had to make do without their doggy condo until I'd constructed another

63

one. It took me about two weeks to finish their new home. When it was done and I put their beds inside, Lulu went and sat on her bed. After about a minute or so, she came over to the open door of my house and offered me a beautiful red and yellow hibiscus flower.

Sadly it was one of the last things she did, as in the next few days she contracted leptospirosis and died. Luckily her sister Nika lived to the ripe old age of 17 years, but I'll never forget Lulu.

By Delpha Menor, Kapaa, Hawaii, United States of America

Mates for life

For some years I reared wild baby birds, rescued and brought to me from around the district. Like most people, I had a mixture of successes and failures. However, one success story, about two blackbirds, stands out from the rest.

As the blackbirds' feathers grew and the female developed a warm brown colouring I realised they were a pair. Once they had learned to fly in the safety of our lounge I released them into the garden, where I continued to feed and support them until they were totally independent. The young male had a white feather on his head and, within days, the female was also easy to distinguish from other blackbirds as she had acquired a droopy wing from a too-close encounter with one of our cats.

The following spring they paired, and so began a productive six-year-long relationship. They often reared two clutches in a season. Until then, I had not realised that wild birds could live so long. They were a constant joy, as they acknowledged my presence by hopping close or calling out unexpectedly from a nearby branch. They always brought their latest fledglings to feed as I scattered the moist morning bread, teaching them to be unafraid of me.

Then, to my sadness, Mum Bird disappeared. At seven years old, it was probably old age. The following spring, Dad Bird paired with a younger female (typical male!) and again raised two clutches. These were to be his last. One day, looking tatty and very tired, he stood within a metre of me on the lawn, stared at me intently while I commiserated with him, and then flew off.

I never saw him again.

By Carol Ercolano, Nelson, New Zealand

And then there were three

This is the tale of a tawny frogmouth affectionately known as Big Bird. I think it shows that wild birds are pretty smart too.

Big Bird came to me one spring, injured, as a lot of birds do (I'm a wildlife carer). After he'd lived in my aviary for several weeks and become very tame, the time came for his release. This presented a dilemma, as I didn't know where he had come from and frogmouths are very territorial.

Another frogmouth started appearing each night and sitting on the clothes line, seemingly besotted with Big Bird, so I finally released him and they flew off together. Time passed, and Big Bird returned and took to sleeping in a particular gum tree in my garden. After about three weeks he disappeared and I thought, 'Oh well, he's moved on.'

One morning I went out and there he was, on the same branch in the same tree. On closer inspection there was not one, not two, but three: dad, mum and a little baby in the middle. They just sat there while I went closer to have a good look. Big Bird had brought his family back to show me. The next day they were gone. He has been back a couple of times since, alone, sitting on the same branch. I think the way he remembers our friendship, even after regaining his freedom, shows that he's pretty smart.

By Kaye McCabe, Deniliquin,
New South Wales, Australia

Write to me ...   ✉

Email Kaye
kmccabe1@bigpond.com.au

Teal's ordeal

One winter, in the days between Christmas and New Year, the heaviest snowfall in living memory left Shetland completely isolated. In the middle of the North Sea, halfway between Britain and Norway, these remote islands – more used to hurricanes than blizzards – suddenly found themselves completely cut off from the outside world. Even the airport was closed.

In sheltered places, drifts were reportedly more than 12 feet deep. And when the snow finally stopped the temperature plummeted, gripping the land in ice. So sudden and unexpected was this freak weather that the national news carried stories of families trapped without food as local shops ran out of supplies.

Alone on the headland where we lived, the view of this winter wonderland was magical. In the days that followed, a pale sun shone out of a clear sky and, all around, the sea was flat as steel. The single-track road that led to our house was impassable and, beyond, the undulating landscape was white and untouched.

So the knock at the back door, when it came, seemed quite out of the blue.

'Do you have a phone I can use?' Breathless, the man in waxed jacket and boots looked distressed. In summer, people usually knocked on our door for free-range eggs or directions. I assumed he'd had an accident. 'I think I need to call the coastguard,' he said. When I asked him what the problem was, his explanation made my blood run cold.

He had walked over from the village with his springer spaniel – but, somewhere along the top of the cliffs, the young dog had slipped and disappeared over the edge. He thought he'd heard barking, so there might still be hope that the dog was alive.

I knew immediately that to call the coastguard volunteers out would take hours and, with the airport closed, the rescue helicopter was probably also out of action. I am not a climber but have scrambled over most of these cliffs. And, with the light fading, time was of the essence. So I threw on a jacket and grabbed a rope from the garage. As a final precaution, I also took a lantern torch and arranged a signal with my wife, who waited back at the house, watching through binoculars: it could prove to be our only lifeline.

Then we set out, plunging through the snow and retracing the man's steps towards the west.

As we skirted the frozen loch the emptiness seemed vast, the silence swallowing our laboured breathing. Finally, we came out at the top of the low sandstone cliff where the tracks disappeared. The sun was setting, and across the Sound the towering bulk of Fitful Head reared up almost a thousand feet out of the sea. Meanwhile, 45 feet below us, the icy waters sucked and gurgled round the base of a rock, as though waiting …

Below, we heard a plaintive bark, then nothing.

Although I knew these cliffs, four feet of snow had rounded and blurred the edges, altering the terrain, and I could no longer be sure. 'What do you think?' the man asked hopefully. Avoiding the flurry of footprints dangerously close to the sheer edge, I lashed myself to one end of the rope and gave him the other. 'Keep this slack, unless you feel a pull.'

67

A little way along the cliff top, I felt sure there was a ledge running down. 'What's his name?' I asked, before ducking from view. 'Teal,' came the answer.

The inclined ledge gave way to a series of outcrops and boulders that eventually led down to the sea. Ordinarily this was an easy descent, but the coating of snow made it precarious: it was also what had broken Teal's fall. As soon as I was underneath the overhang, it became clear what had happened. Skittering over the edge, Teal had half-fallen, half-bounded down three different levels, ending up on a snow-covered rock eight feet above the water. If the sea hadn't been calm, he could have been washed straight off. But he just sat there, apparently unhurt, barking and thumping his tail.

The trickiest part was scrambling over onto his rock. There, balanced above the cold clear waters, I had a momentary vision of him refusing to come with me, retreating nervously, and finally both of us ending up in the sea. But Teal was made of good obedient stuff: he waited, patiently bundled into my arms, as I shrugged him into the most comfortable position for our climb out. 'Got him! Now, keep the rope taut!' I shouted up.

Once this was done, we tottered, teetered and crawled our way up the cliff – not a bad effort, with no hands! Teal, happy to be rescued, cooperated by becoming as limp as a sack of potatoes against my chest. I talked to him as he licked my chin, while trying to blot out all thoughts of the empty space at our backs.

The most nerve-wrenching – and hazardous – part of the operation came at the top. Planting my feet on a narrow ledge below the overhang, I had to lift him at full stretch and toss him clear. He never even wriggled. Two minutes later, I clambered up after him and we were home free. At the top, dog and owner were happily reunited. We checked him over, and found that lucky Teal hadn't even a scratch from his ordeal.

We retreated a few steps and chatted, elated, while coiling the rope and admiring the view. The sun had gone down and the sea was flat as slate, darkening the distant cliffs. The landscape seemed polar – remote from civilisation. And we felt like Arctic explorers who had just triumphed over the odds. But Teal, sitting a distance away, seemed subdued.

Suddenly, he jumped up with a bark. In that split second, we felt the ground give way as the cornice we were standing on collapsed. With a sickening lurch, the world seemed to turn upside down as I waited for the bottomless drop. It never came: we had fallen through the crust and come to an abrupt halt just above our knees. We turned to each other, then – without a word – gingerly extricated ourselves and carefully tiptoed over towards Teal, 12 feet back on solid ground.

His expression said quite plainly that, having been over the edge once, he would not be rushing to repeat his experience. Good old Teal. Somehow, I don't think I blame him for getting cold feet.

By Gary Wright, London, England

Home at last

My mother had just moved into a seven-storey apartment building and was taking out a bag of garbage when she first saw Little Girl. She was a tiny black and white cat who was very timid – and very hungry. She was getting scraps out of the dumpster and living in the bushes behind the building.

For the next few months, Mom would see the little cat every day. She began to take down canned cat food for her. Little Girl would wait for Mom to give the signal (which was jingling her car keys) and out she would come, mewing and rubbing against Mom's legs.

69

No one else could get close to Little Girl, although there were many well-meaning people who tried. But Little Girl had chosen my mom. Mom began to worry about the approaching winter. How would Little Girl survive the cold?

One day when Mom came home from work, she spotted Little Girl sitting in Mom's parking space outside the apartment building. Her neighbour told her that Little Girl had sat there all night, crying, looking up at Mom's apartment on the sixth floor. Little Girl even knew which apartment Mom lived in! Mom was so touched and amazed that she decided to take Little Girl home.

Little Girl has been with Mom for two years now, and Mom has never regretted taking her in. From the first moment Little Girl walked into the apartment, it was as if she was finally home.

By Michelle Vansickle, Sarnia, Ontario, Canada

Bob to the rescue

I am a volunteer wildlife rescuer. Several years ago, I was looking after four baby ringtail possums who ranged in weight from 50 to 80 grams. At this size they needed to be fed three to four times a day on a special lactose-free milk formula. They lived in a hand-knitted pouch in a basket that is kept warm at a regular temperature.

When feeding time came and I opened the basket it was impossible to pick out each possum one at a time because, before I knew what was happening, they all scampered up my arm. They have sharp little claws (for climbing trees in the wild), and they thought nothing of making full use of them to make sure they didn't fall off me while they waited to be fed individually. Their favourite spot was nestling at the highest point – my head – where they clung happily to my hair and scalp.

You can imagine that, after several days of this, I was getting quite desperate to find a substitute! I thought for a moment, and while I was looking around it suddenly came to me – there, sitting on the shelf, was my teddy bear, Bob. Why hadn't I thought of it sooner? I picked up Bob, who is a large plush bear. He has good old reliable 'hugability' and is not one of the prima donna mohair limited edition types who would be terribly put out by all this nonsense.

At the next feeding time for the possums I placed Bob at the opening of the basket and, to my immense delight and relief, all four fluff-balls scampered onto him and clung lovingly to his fur. I was safe!

Postscript: All four of the baby possums thrived in foster care and were released back into the wild several months later.

By Leslie Breackell, North Sydney, New South Wales, Australia

A matter of trust

It all started one afternoon when I rescued a honeyeater from our neighbour's cat's mouth. The poor bird was not wounded, but I was worried he would go into shock. As it was getting dark, I decided it would be best to release the bird the next day when I got home from work – if he survived.

I carefully placed him into an old home-made cat cage with an array of small branches and some water, and left him in a dark room. When I checked on him before I went to bed, and again in the morning, I was happy to see he was still alive and well.

However, when I arrived home from work that day, I was horrified to find that the door to the room where I was keeping the bird was open. As there were three cats in the house, my blood pressure went up. I thought he must have died during the day, but my mum

71

said no, she thought I had already let him go early in the morning because, when she went to check on him, he wasn't there.

I went into the bedroom and shut the door, looking everywhere. I realised there were gaps in the cage that the little honeyeater could easily have squeezed through, and that he must be in the house somewhere. That's when I saw him, perched on a clown wig which was hanging on the wall, looking at me intently.

What happened next surprised me, as I thought it was ridiculous to even try it – but it worked. I held my finger out to him, and he calmly walked onto it. Then I put him back into the cage, which he willingly let me do – it was unbelievable.

I walked out into the garden and placed the cage on the lawn, then opened the cage door and once again held out my finger to him. He hopped onto it, and I carefully set him down on top of the cage. I said, 'Well, you're free to go any time you want, little fella.' He cocked his head, looked at me, then chirped for quite a while, like he was telling me a story. I'd like to think he was thanking me. Then he flew off, chirping noisily to let his mates know he was back.

It was just one of those amazing moments that you feel really lucky to experience; something that will always stay with me.

Later that day as I was feeding my horses, three different people came up to me and asked what was up with me, 'because you haven't been able to wipe the smile off your face all afternoon!'

Isn't it fantastic that one so small can have such an impact on one so much larger. I hope he is still out there living a happy life.

By Karen Mol, Perth,
Western Australia

Write to me …

Karen Mol
7d Chailey Place
Balga, Perth, WA 6061
Australia
email: misslestat@hotmail.com

Rescued animal photos

Darbi assesses the situation (story on page 1)

Photo provided by Kim Lopes

Is Chevy thinking about good bone hiding places? (story on page 2)

Photo provided by Justine O'Leary

Resourceful Whiskey (story on page 3)

Photo provided by Gina Sturkenboom

Photo provided by Barbara Bryan

Heroic Sasha (story on page 11)

Photo provided by Carol King

Ludo the cat and Homeboy the pigeon resting together (story on page 17)

75

Bumpus O'Beast stores energy for his 'rat dance' (story on page 25)

Photo provided by Charlotte Stanley

Photo provided by Sarah McIntosh

Men will come and go but Phoebe's here to stay (story on page 21)

Photo provided by John Litchen

Observant Shady (story on page 31)

Photo provided by Hearing Dogs for Deaf People

Janet and Gypsy (story on page 36)

Photo provided by Suzanne Post

Having only three legs is no barrier to Sasha (story on page 38)

Photo provided by Nikki Harris

Nikki and Delta (story on page 44)

Photo provided by Hearing Dogs for Deaf People

Mags and Taz (story on page 48)

Photo provided by Myra Taankink

Tyson looks for company (story on page 50)

Photo provided by Karen Mol

Biskit chose the right doorstep (story on page 56)

81

Happy Henry the lorikeet (story on page 89)

Kerry and Zulu (story on page 90)

Photo provided by Dani de la Mare

Bert and Bob (story on page 94)

Photo provided by Marlene Beck

Sweet Polly (story on page 96)

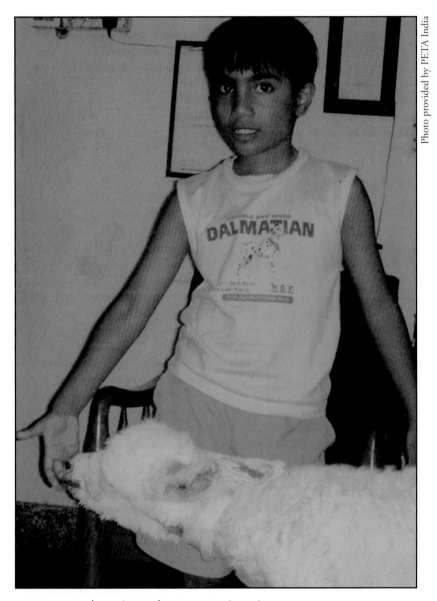

Zubin and one of his many animal friends (story on page 138)

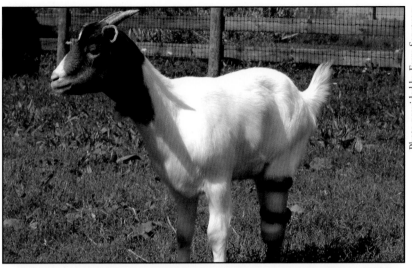

Photo provided by Farm Sanctuary

Juniper complete with her special leg (story on page 133)

Photo provided by Deborah Lafata

Toby is restored to good health (story on page 140)

The smartest animal of all!

Many of our readers love to take photos of their pets reading (or sleeping on) SMARTER than JACK books – now, that is smart! We love getting these pictures and thought they should no longer be kept hidden from public view. In each edition of SMARTER than JACK we will publish the best new photo we have received.

For submission information please go to page 148.

This photo of Donsje is by Marguerite Vlielander of Brasschaat, Belgium. Marguerite receives a complimentary copy of this book.

Donsje indicates which book she likes best

Your say . . .

Here at SMARTER than JACK we love reading the mail we receive from people who have been involved with our books. This mail includes letters from both contributors and readers. We thought we would share with you excerpts from some of the letters that really touched our hearts.

'I really love the book "Heroic animals are SMARTER than JACK". It is one of the best books I have ever read. It was so sad that Susie died saving Bridget and her sister from a rabid dog in Pakistan (in the story "We'll never forget Susie"). I had tears in my eyes.

I am a vegetarian and a true animal lover. Good luck with more books – I can't wait to read them!'

Asia (aged 9), New Zealand

Penny the dog by Abby, aged 7
(story on page 4)

'Thanks for such great books. You are creating more than a fundraiser, you are creating a history of the animal world. It is unique.'

Jill, Canada

'I loved reading the latest SMARTER than JACK. Isn't it good to know there are so many people all over the world who really love their pets!'

Bridget, England

'I recently finished reading my first SMARTER than JACK book, which I ordered through my PETA membership newsletter. The stories were GREAT.

I also have to commend you people for donating some of the proceeds to humane associations.'

Charllyce, United States of America

'Thank you all so much for the wonderful SMARTER than JACK book which I received today, featuring myself and Jinty. Everyone that I've shown it to thinks that it is a book worth having – so many true stories. It's marvellous what animals will do to help their owners.

Keep up the good work. I shall look forward to the next issue which I will definitely buy.'

Ann, England

'I love the stories and have emailed them to friends, relatives and past students. It's encouraging to hear of others who care deeply for animals and recognise their intelligence and nobility.'

Collette, Canada

'I received my copy of "Cheeky animals are SMARTER than JACK" and I am so thrilled to see my cheeky hound in print! ... Please keep them coming, they are so enjoyable as well as amusing and heart-warming.'

Maureen, Australia

'I have read the whole book now and cannot wait to find time to read it all again – so interesting ... Long may SMARTER than JACK reign glorious.'

Gwen, New Zealand

6

Rescued animals triumph over adversity

Happy Henry

photo p82

I got a call from our 'rescue' office to pick up a rainbow lorikeet who was unable to fly. When I arrived to get him, he was huddled on the ground looking very sorry for himself. I checked him over and then took him to a vet to see what might be wrong. Somehow he had injured his shoulder quite badly and he needed lots of rest and recuperation.

Now, I have known some feisty lorikeets in my 'rescue' years, but Henry (as I came to call him) was different right from the beginning. He was the most trusting bird I had ever come across. He endured his daily wing physiotherapy with only the slightest annoyance. But, as the days went by, there didn't seem to be any real improvement. Every time he tried to launch himself for flight, he'd drop like a lead balloon. After many months, he became known as my 'special needs' bird and managed perfectly well despite his handicap, getting around by walking, hopping and climbing.

He amazes everyone by being a 'normal' bird in every other way except he cannot fly. He still gets up to everything other lorikeets do – including attracting a mate. At Christmas time another lorikeet came visiting, and she liked Henry so much that she has never left.

89

Henry has shown us how a bird can thrive on care and love from good friends – and that you don't need to fly to be a happy bird.

By Leslie Breackell, North Sydney, New South Wales, Australia

Zulu's hope

He was full-grown. Black. Wild. Out of control. A beautiful Dobermann/Lab cross who was purchased at a pet store, endured seven miserable months of his puppyhood on a backyard chain, and was then relinquished to the Nebraska Humane Society to languish for six long months in an adoption kennel.

From the moment I saw this brindle-pawed beauty, his pleading eyes held a promise. I had no idea what was to come, but I was smitten by his exuberant personality in spite of his circumstances.

Because he was a 'long-term' dog, his adoption fee was reduced to a mere $37.50. A beautiful life for the cost of filling my gas tank. He was beginning to demonstrate those fateful behaviours of mental deterioration that all animals will exhibit when housed for too long in abnormal conditions: tail chasing, frenetic pacing and erratic jumping. These were signs that something had to be done – and quickly. I wanted to save him and give him a second chance at life.

So I made the commitment to love him for the rest of his life and we went home together – two souls embarking on a new journey. What I quickly discovered was that he was filled with not only abounding love but also a terrible fear of feet, loud noises and raised voices. Clear signs of abuse. Immediately, I changed his name to Zulu so that he could begin his life anew. I promised him he would never again know pain as long as he was with me.

We never looked back from that day forward, and our bond grew stronger with each passing day. Zulu blossomed into a strong, confident and obedient dog. He demonstrated such potential that he began to train as an assistance dog, so that he and I could go out and teach others about the amazing human/animal bond and the potential of all shelter dogs.

After three months, Zulu proudly earned his title of 'Professional Certified Therapy Dog'. Together, we visit thousands of people, both young and old, to share Zulu's story of his journey from abuse and abandonment to adoption and adoration. Zulu's gentle demeanour and love for everyone shows others a better way: the power and peace that comes with forgiveness and acceptance. He demonstrates to at-risk kids that we can overcome bad circumstances.

Zulu possesses the magical ability to make everyone he meets a little more tender, a little more loving, a little more human. That was the promise he held in his eyes.

By Kerry Ecklebe,
Nebraska Humane Society,
Omaha, Nebraska,
United States of America

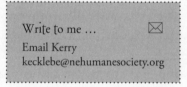

Write to me …

Email Kerry
kecklebe@nehumanesociety.org

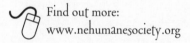

Find out more:
www.nehumanesociety.org

A special bunny

On weekends I usually like to sleep late in the mornings, so when my husband Ted woke me from a deep sleep at 6 am on a Sunday I was less than happy. However, when I heard the words 'You need to come with me and bring the carrier, I think Black Bunny is hurt' I sprang out of bed like it was nearly noon.

'Little Black Bunny' was what we had affectionately named the stray rabbit who'd suddenly appeared in our neighbourhood shortly after Easter 1999. He looked like a young male. He was jet black, so we knew he was not wild. He would come to 'visit' our pet rabbits – two Dutch bunnies, Cinnamon and Raindrop – when they were in their outdoor hutch. They were indoor rabbits, but we would put them outside for the day when the weather was good.

Black Bunny would also go round to other yards, provided the people there would treat him to a piece of carrot or a sliver of apple. However, he would never let anyone get closer than an arm's length away. If he had, he would have been welcomed into our family much sooner.

Then came that frightening March morning, nearly a year after he had first appeared. Ted had been out jogging, and he happened to see Black Bunny on the side of the road. He looked like he had been hit by a car. But, when Ted approached him, he moved – actually, more like rolled – under a parked car, then out the other side. That's when Ted ran home to get me. We managed to pick up Black Bunny, put him in the carrier and get him to Animerge, a local after-hours emergency veterinary clinic.

The vet on call knew immediately what was wrong. Black Bunny suffered from an untreated ear infection that caused scar tissue to form on his inner ear and brain, causing him to lose his equilibrium. The vet was not sure if it could cured, and asked us to make a decision on his fate. Of course, we decided to give him a chance. He had apparently been tossed aside once already in his short innocent life, and we were not about to abandon him as someone else had done.

We took him home, set him up in a cage with soft carpet walls, administered antibiotics and gave him endless amounts of love. Over time, Black Bunny seemed to learn to control his off-balance rolling, having the most trouble with it when he was tired or was being

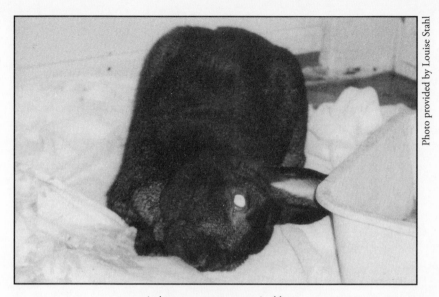

Photo provided by Louise Stahl

Black Bunny: a very special rabbit

picked up. His head was always cocked to one side, and we believe he'd lost sight in the eye on the downward-facing side.

He became our 'handicapped bunny', and taught my young niece to treat creatures less fortunate than others with a little bit of extra care and concern. He became fast friends with Cinnamon and Raindrop. He ate heartily and soon became *Big* Black Bunny. And, for all his troubles, he always had a sparkle in his one good eye.

Unfortunately, just last autumn the infection that had settled in his ear came back and affected his bladder and urinary tract. The vet we took him to at the end did not know his story, and only saw him as a rabbit who had just contracted an illness which caused him to roll almost uncontrollably. He told me that Black Bunny would never be normal, would never stop rolling and would not survive. I informed him that Black Bunny had been that way for five years, yet he had conquered his disability to hop with the other bunnies – only with a little more 'walk' than 'hop' in his step. The vet looked at me and said, 'Well, you must have taken very good care of him.' How could I not? He gave unconditional love and overcame adversity in so many ways.

Now that he is gone, I am thankful he was such a fighter and that he trusted us enough to let us bring him into our home and our family. He was a special little fellow, who took a little bit of our hearts with him into heaven but left a lot of himself here with us.

By Louise Stahl, Somerville, New Jersey, United States of America

Write to me …

Email Louise
louisestahl2001@yahoo.com

Bert the wonder dog: a tale of survival

photo
p83

I had always wanted acreage in the country so that I could have lots of animals. I loved all kinds of critters and I started giving homes to other people's cast-offs. First came two kittens (I had to promise my husband they would be barn kittens – that lasted until the first cold night). Then came the chickens. Two more kittens found their way to us, again to be barn cats. The horse stepped on one kitten's paw, so that was it – up to the house they moved. We already had a 40-year-old pony, a young Arabian gelding and my old black Labrador.

One day my girlfriend and I were driving along a stretch of road that was forested on both sides. I yelled at her to stop, for there at the side of the road sat the homeliest, scrawniest, most lost-looking puppy I had ever seen.

After coaxing my friend to turn the car around, I jumped out and walked towards him, but as I approached he turned and ran into the bush. Thinking he was a wild puppy, I followed him to see where he was headed. The little guy led me through the bush to his two sick little brothers. There, against an old brick hut, they lay. One was covered from the waist down with his own faeces, while the other was so thin he looked like an emaciated goat. It was the most pathetic sight I had seen, the two of them huddled there. Then there was Bert, as I named the first puppy I'd seen, the wonder dog who had led me to them. He had sat on that quiet road just waiting for someone to stop and rescue the three of them.

Without even thinking, I scooped them all up in my arms and headed for my friend's car. When I arrived home my husband just stared at me, sitting there in the car with three seemingly lifeless puppies on my lap. After much care, nourishment and several visits to the vet, they grew from pups who looked like little old men in puppies' bodies into beautiful thriving young dogs.

Three growing dogs proved too much to handle, and I sadly realised that I would have to part with one. It was a very hard decision, but in the end I found a good home for the blonde one and kept the two curly long-coated boys: Bert and Bob.

Bert remained strong, confident and so smart that he sometimes scared me. Bob, on the other hand, is insecure, spacey and a real mommy's boy. They are 12 and a half years old now and I adore them more than I would ever have expected to.

By Dani de la Mare, Aldergrove,
British Columbia, Canada

Write to me … ✉

Dani de la Mare
25065 Robertson Crescent
Aldergrove, BC V4W 1W7
Canada
email: dani.delamare@shaw.ca

photo
p83

An old dog learns new tricks

Polly was a 'rescue' dog, a little white Jack Russell. When we first saw her she was a sorry sight. She was almost deaf and partially blind, and her ears had been eaten away by an untreated illness. But we could not resist her, even though she was elderly (about 14 years old) and not long for this world.

When we got her home, we realised the extent of her mistreatment by the fact that she made no noise at all. She tried to crawl into the corner of the shed to sleep on newspapers and would not enter the house.

In the two years we had her, she learnt everything a puppy learns. She learnt how to run, to sit and wait for her food, and at last – after almost six months – how to bark. The first day I came home and she ran to greet me barking was one of the highlights of my life.

Maybe she didn't do anything spectacular in the two years she had left of her life, but she did learn to be a dog – a dog that was loved to bits. After a really rough start she ended her life very happy.

By Marlene Beck, Leicester,
England

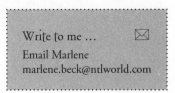
Write to me …
Email Marlene
marlene.beck@ntlworld.com

Out for a duck

'Duck Down' was our cottage beside a bubbling stream. Here we created a bird sanctuary, treating injured and orphaned birds, especially ducklings. Locals called us the 'Quack Doctors' and brought us many feathered patients.

Hoppy was one such patient. She had been snatched from the jaws of a conger eel soon after hatching, and one leg was ripped off.

She was in shock and very weak. We nestled her under a suspended rag mop (a good substitute mother) on a heated pad. I nursed her for weeks, admiring her pluck as she held on to life. We fed her egg yolk and cereal, Jellimeat, worms and water weed. Soon she was hopping round the garden with me, guzzling coffee from my cup – and leaving grass clippings as evidence!

We oiled her soft down as her mother would do, and watched her first struggles to swim. When her feathers grew to replace baby down, it was time to help her hop and flap her wings for balance. She grew stronger, learning the fun of flapping up a windstorm and lurching forward on her one leg.

The day came for Hoppy's maiden flight. With some regret, we bade her farewell and released her. Hoppy hopped along the bank, furiously flapping her tiny wings, then raised her undercarriage and took off. She circled our home many times as if learning her location, before crashing back beside me, exhausted.

This routine went on for several weeks. Then, one day, Hoppy soared above us, quacked her farewell, and was away to seek her fortune. Her visits home became less frequent, but when she did return it was delightful as she made such a fuss of us.

Winter came, and no sign of Hoppy. We thought her disability had made her easy prey to some hungry animal. Imagine our delight the following spring when our dear familiar, awkward, low-flying duck swooped over us in the garden. Ducking down, I could feel the wind of powerful beating wings. Hoppy crash-landed clumsily on the lawn, nosedived, then regained her balance. She viewed us coyly with her head on one side, chattering happily.

We became aware of another duck, who now performed an identical circuit and crash-landed beside Hoppy. Together they hobbled and hopped up the bank to my feet. Hoppy had come home, and she had brought her boyfriend to meet the family. Hopalong is a

97

handsome young mallard with lustrous plumage – and one leg! They are perfectly matched, and I'm sure they will live happily ever after.

By Rosemary Francis, Kaiapoi, North Canterbury, New Zealand

Just look for the sparkle

Bun Bun was a brave bunny soul who had lost the use of her hind limbs. I met her while doing my small-animal internship at the University of Pennsylvania Veterinary Hospital. When my shift was over for the day, I would go through the wards looking for hospitalised bunnies to give some special attention to. I found Bun Bun in a cage with a blanket wrapped around one of her hind legs.

According to her medical chart, Bun Bun was a happy, healthy eight-year-old spayed white and grey female house rabbit who had previously enjoyed walks in the park and travelling. So why couldn't she use her hind legs any more? A battery of tests revealed she had discospondylitis, an inflammation of a spinal vertebra and disc. She was sent home with medication for the inflammation and orders for home physical therapy. I worried about her and wondered how she was doing.

A few weeks later, I saw flyers around the hospital seeking an experienced rabbit person to care for an elderly sickly bun while her owner went away on vacation. Wouldn't you know it, it was the owner of Bun Bun!

I got the 'job' and met Bun Bun again at the hospital. She now had no use of her hind legs at all. Once I got her home, I looked her over. She seemed to be in good condition and not depressed by her current state – I looked into her eyes and saw a sparkle. But her joints were really stiff, and it was obvious that her owner didn't work her joints and muscles well enough to keep them from freezing up.

To make Bun Bun feel as involved in life as I could, I carried her with me everywhere around home – studying on the floor, watching TV on the couch and working on the computer.

I also manipulated her joints and muscles every chance I got. I wanted to see if she could regain some movement in her hind legs. After a while she got limber enough to be 'frog-legged' – holding her back legs out behind her, but not perfectly straight – and we could position her legs differently to vary her level of comfort.

Bun Bun slept in a box that lay on its side on the floor. Now when I checked on her in the mornings, she was no longer in her box. The determined little girl had started dragging her body out of her box during the night to see what else was out there.

Okay, so this girl *wanted* to move. Fine, I could help her with that. I got a towel and placed the little rabbit in a towel sling. Starting at one end of the hallway, I lifted and supported her hind end and off she went, motoring down the hallway on her front legs. She was elated! Now we could make her *walk* to the room we were sitting in. No more pitiful paralysed Bun Bun.

Her mom returned from her vacation and we made plans to have Bun Bun go home. But then the 9/11 tragedy took place, and Bun Bun's mom had family in the Towers. She called and asked if I could keep Bun Bun a little while longer. I was sad to hear of her personal loss, but happy to spend more time with Bun Bun.

At this time my small-animal internship at the hospital was ending and I had to move on to the University's large-animal facility, two hours from home, for the second half of my internship. Fortunately Cathy, a good friend and a volunteer at our House Rabbit Society, offered to let me and Bun Bun live in her home, only 20 minutes away from the large-animal facility, during my three-month internship.

At Cathy's house we decided to make Bun Bun a 'wheelchair' so that she could move around without my help. It had to be comfortable and lightweight, and needed to be something she could rest her front legs on when she got tired. We started with a skateboard, and eventually – with a lot of alteration, trial and error, innovation and persistence – Bun Bun had wheels that meant she could walk and rest as she pleased.

I'd thought she was happy when she first started to towel-walk – but you should have seen her now, zipping all over the place!

One day Cathy found that Bun Bun had wheeled down a short hallway off the kitchen, 'jumped' herself and her wheelchair down one step and was now in the family room looking for Cathy's bunny, Watson. Nothing was going to stop this girl!

Weeks turned into months, and Bun Bun was still living with me. My large-animal internship finished, and I moved back home with my little girl. She met and fell in love with one of my other bunnies, Floppy, and they spent a lot of time together.

I worked at a vet's office and took her to work with me each day so she wouldn't be bored or depressed. Everyone was amazed by this bunny in a wheelchair. My co-workers enjoyed feeding her the 'allowed veggies' that I packed for her every morning.

Then one day I noticed that Bun Bun didn't want to wheel herself very far. I picked her up and examined her. She had a lump on her elbow, which turned out to be an abscess on her elbow joint. The vet suggested surgery, but I was torn – she was almost nine years old and had been through so much already. She was on antibiotics and I was still deciding what to do. Then I noticed her getting sicker and lethargic – too sick for anaesthesia and surgery. So I kept her as comfortable as possible and then one night, when she was in a lot of pain, I had her put to sleep.

I hope Bun Bun's story will inspire you to look at those who are differently-abled – humans and animals – as beautiful living souls. Just because they can't do certain things it doesn't mean they don't have the will and the desire to enjoy life. Look into their eyes and you will see that sparkle.

By Ronita Lawrence, Allentown,
Pennsylvania, United States of America

Write to me … ✉
Email Ronita (Ronie)
roniebunny@aol.com

Saved from the flames: the story of a survivor

June 12, 1996 was a hot summer day in Houston, Texas. In a small town outside this big city, a teenage boy spotted a homeless dog wandering through his neighbourhood. He quickly discovered that this lovely stray was also sweet as she came up to him right away, walking with a limp. Her paw had been injured, no doubt as a result of a hard life on the streets.

This nameless dog would some day be Burnadette – also known as Burnie – but now she was a nameless orphan, and she was afraid, sick and desperate for attention. There is no doubt this lonely dog thought she had found a new friend and perhaps a lifelong home when this young man took her in and asked his parents if he could keep her. Burnie's long tail must have been wagging like crazy as the boy put a rope around her neck for a leash and walked her over to a friend's house. What happened next is almost too horrible to imagine – but it did, and Burnie still bears the scars to prove it.

Burnie's excitement at finding companionship quickly turned to panic as the two teens slowly began to douse her skinny body with gasoline, then lit a match and tossed it at her. As the stray dog burned and writhed in agony, the boys watched with a strange sense of fascination.

101

Burnie fought to end the pain. She scorched her mouth and tongue and lost most of her whiskers as she tried to bite at the flames. She limped away, dragging the rope still tied around her neck. A neighbour saw the dog, still on fire, and turned the garden hose on her to extinguish the flames. By the time the fire had been put out, Burnie had received serious second- and third-degree burns that covered over 40 per cent of her body. A kind and caring animal control officer arrived after a neighbour called the police.

The animal control officer, surveying Burnie's grave condition, called on the Houston Humane Society (HHS) to begin the long road of treatments and medical care. The two young men who committed this horrific act have been caught – although they were only forced to pay a fine, as happens in most animal cruelty cases.

A decade later Burnie still bears scars, but she is healed in every other way. She is the HHS mascot, and has finally discovered what it's like to have the love of a family. She travels with HHS animal cruelty officers to schools, teaching children about animal cruelty, and she lends her loving paw to all of the activities at the shelter.

Despite everything that has happened to Burnie, she still absolutely loves people. Meeting this friendly, energetic and affectionate dog, one would never guess the nightmare she endured.

Burnie is truly an amazing dog. She has touched all our lives, and serves as a shining example of what can be accomplished with a lot of love, a little courage and a strong will to live.

By Courtney Frank,
Houston Humane Society,
Houston, Texas,
United States of America

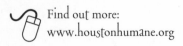 Find out more:
www.houstonhumane.org

Write to me … ✉

Burnie
Houston Humane Society
14700 Almeda Road
Houston, TX 77053
USA

7

Rescued animals have fun

Bums the ball player

Our Siamese cat Bums was so named because he had been found wandering along the side of a freeway by a policeman friend out on highway patrol. Our friend knew we had several Siamese cats, and correctly thought we wouldn't mind accepting another member into the gang.

Bums soon confiscated our youngest daughter's tiny ball (normally used for playing the game 'jacks') as his. When he wasn't using it, he kept it well hidden so that she and the rest of us could not locate it.

Every Wednesday I cleaned two of the upstairs bedrooms and this job usually took me about an hour. I had to open the hallway door to go upstairs, and Bums was already waiting for me at the door with the ball in his mouth when I arrived with the vacuum cleaner, clean sheets, etc. As soon as the door was opened he raced up the stairs, chewing hard on his ball.

He would spend the entire time I was cleaning the upstairs bedrooms dropping the ball down the stairs, watching it like a hawk as it bounced down each step. When the ball reached the last step he literally flew down the stairs – it didn't look like his feet touched even one step – and grabbed it fiercely in his mouth before it touched the hallway floor. When he grew tired, he would rest at the top of the stairs with the ball between his paws, watching it intently just in case it should try to escape his clutches. Every once in a while he would hit it with his paws and chew it hard so that the ball knew who was boss, and then he would start the ball game all over again.

When I was finished cleaning, he took the ball in his mouth and walked downstairs with me. He would put the ball away in his secret hiding place until next Wednesday, when he would be waiting by the door again for another ball game.

By Eileen Ohrling, North Vancouver, British Columbia, Canada

Precious and playful

I found my precious baby boy Hobo at the SPCA in Hamilton. He was a timid little tabby kitten, about six months old. He'd had a rough start in life, being abandoned and living rough on the streets until he was rescued by the SPCA.

I think it was love at first sight for both of us. And, as so often happens, he chose me before I chose him. I was working at the SPCA as a volunteer, and every day I went in he was waiting at the front of the cage for me. He didn't take any great notice of the other staff there, or of visitors, but he would come running when he heard my voice. I grew very fond of him, and the day came when I could no longer bear to leave him in the cage at the end of the day so he came home with me.

Hobo – so named because of his early life on the streets – settled in very quickly, and soon his boisterous playful side shone through. I had a rather large plastic bowl on the lounge floor that I would put a ping-pong ball into, and Hobo would jump in and chase the ball round and round for hours. If the ball dared to escape from the bowl, he would chase it round the house until he found me and he'd then look up at me and meow until I returned it to the bowl.

Hobo was also fascinated by fireworks. He would sit on the windowsill and watch them for hours. Sometimes if a car backfired, he would think it was fireworks time again and would run to the window and look out hopefully, only to be disappointed when he couldn't see any lights in the sky.

One of Hobo's other tricks was that he would wait by the mailbox for me if I had gone out in my car. He seemed to know the sound of my car, and as I pulled into the driveway he would jump up, run over to the car and wait till I opened the door so that he could climb in. He did this every day without fail and would happily ride up the driveway with me, on the passenger seat. One day he wouldn't get out of the car, so when I went out again he came to the supermarket with me!

Sadly, Hobo was not a well young lad and he passed away when he was just a few years old. I will never forget the time I had with him, and thinking of his antics still brings a smile to my face!

By Lisa Fowler, Tauranga,
New Zealand

Write to me … ✉

Email Lisa
lisaf@kol.co.nz

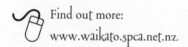 Find out more:
www.waikato.spca.net.nz

Getting to know Buster

Buster the cockatiel was a survivor by circumstance. A great bush fire tragedy had resulted in her human family perishing in their home. At the time of the fire Buster was being looked after by a relative, who had been minding her while her human family had been away and had yet to return her home.

All of the family's other pets had also perished in the fire – except their horse, who had escaped when a passer-by released him from his paddock, and Buster.

Buster needed a new home, and my husband and I were grateful for the chance to let her join our family. Getting to know this tame little bird was a journey of discovery as we learned her endearing quirky little behaviours – such as wanting to share our showers and 'helping' to unpack the groceries after a shopping trip.

Buster took a little while to get to know us and she was very quiet for some weeks. The turning point came when she was sitting on my shoulder one day and the song *California Dreaming* by the Mamas and the Papas started playing on the stereo. The music must have triggered something in her memory, as she immediately began to whistle along and dance joyfully to the music. What a delight to have discovered something familiar to her!

As soon as the song had finished, Buster again fell silent. Consequently we played that song an awful lot as it gave us great joy to watch Buster sing and dance. We bonded over this song and, even though we experimented with other fun tunes, *California Dreaming* remained everyone's firm favourite.

By Julie Raverty, Echuca, Victoria, Australia

The copycat

I rescued my long-haired dark tortie Bella from a pet shop about three years ago.

She had been turned out from her original home after becoming pregnant with her first litter at about ten months of age. She had six of the most beautiful kittens, which had been taken away from her and placed in a cage for sale at the pet shop. Bella was in a larger cage

Photo provided by Julie Raverty

Who's a pretty boy then? Buster, of course.

on the floor. This meant she was in full view of the kittens, and they were calling to each other all the time. It seemed so cruel.

I asked the pet shop to spay her, worm her and attend to any fleas, and said I would take her home for a four-week trial. As soon as she entered my home she fled under the sofa and did not want to come out. She was frightened of anyone who came into the house and would hide away.

Gradually, she came to trust me. As she was long-haired, I needed to groom her often. She began to come to me when she saw the brush and comb. Then came the day when she would actually be waiting for me to get on with the job. With such a pleading look in her eyes, I could not refuse to do it there and then.

After a week or two I decided it was safe to let her outside and that she wouldn't wander too far. I tried to teach her to use the cat door in my laundry. First, I went outside with some food to tempt her, but no way was she going to put her head into that small hole. Then I sat on the floor next to her and repeatedly pushed the flap with my right hand to show her how it opened. For a while she didn't show any response, then suddenly she looked up at me (she has the most lovely eyes) and, using her right paw, she copied what I had been doing – opening the flap with her paw instead of her head – then went outside. Hooray, success at last! Now, she always uses the cat flap – unless I am in the kitchen as she knows I am a softie and will open the door for her.

She is now a keen gardener. When I weed and dig the garden she will sit beside me and dig over the area I have already tidied, then sit and look at me. When I prune a shrub she reaches up and pulls down a branch from another plant, and when I cut off the necessary part she bites off the end of the stalk or branch she has grabbed. If she is asleep indoors and I go out into the garden, she wakes up in seconds and comes outside to keep me company. When I come indoors she follows me. It's like having a shadow.

She likes to play ping-pong with me across the lounge. Standing on her hind legs, she uses both paws to pat the ball back to me – all with no training. Believe it or not, I can leave knitting wool, sewing or anything on the chair or floor – even during the night – and she never touches anything. She just plays with her own toys, leaving me to clear them all up from the hall floor each morning.

Bella is just such a loving and cuddly companion and I often wonder if she remembers her cruel and neglected youth.

By Gwen Keene, Upper Hutt, New Zealand

A canine caper

My sister Jane has two formerly stray dogs, Sadie and Dave. Sadie is the leader of the pack and is always getting Dave into trouble. Jane will sometimes hide behind the back door and, when Sadie comes in from the backyard, she'll jump out and say, 'Boo!'

One afternoon, after Jane had jumped out at Sadie, Sadie ran behind the door. Then, as Dave walked in, she jumped out at him and said, *Woof!*

By Mary Perona, Cashiers, North Carolina, United States of America

My friend the mousebird

Peepee came into my life when I was 14. My sister and her friend found him while they were walking home from school. They placed him in a box labelled 'Belly' on my bed.

109

'What's this?' I asked my sister as she walked past my room.

'A baby bird,' she said simply. 'A very greedy and hungry baby bird.'

So I opened the box, not realising that this was the start of a friendship that would last for many years. I lifted the lid and stared straight into the open beak of a cheeky-looking, almost featherless, fat pink bird. His only feathers were the feathers that crowned his head.

Peepee turned out to be a mousebird. Mousebirds live in large social groups and so it was only natural that Peepee would think of our family as his flock. He considered himself human and flaunted his hierarchy over our ringneck parrots. It's not hard to understand why he believed he was human – he drank out of cups, ate off our plates, played hide-and-seek with us and slept in a shoebox under a small knitted blanket. (Mousebirds can't perch like other birds, they hang from objects instead – hence his sleeping in a box.)

The crown of feathers on his head would rise and fall in curiosity every time he saw something of interest, and he'd do this ridiculous little thing I called a 'mouse dance' on the floor, where he would shuffle along the floor like a wind-up mouse. This was an instinct. Wild mousebirds love sand baths and he was merely imitating this behaviour.

The worst part of Peepee's day was bedtime – he hated bedtimes. He waited for the usual bedtime cues and promptly hid. We would call his name and there would be no sign of him. There are only so many hiding places in a home and eventually we became master 'Peepee hunters', looking in all his favourite spots as we searched for the little time-waster. He liked hiding among the hanging cutlery in the kitchen, or burying himself under the sweaters in the sweater cupboard, or sitting dead still among my mother's ornaments on top of the pelmet. Just when we thought we had all his hiding places sussed, he found another one.

In high school I was called the 'Bird Girl', and the other girls would bring me baby birds and expect me to work miracles. I had always tried my best, but my success rate really went up after I befriended Peepee. I would get a baby bird and take it home and, no matter what kind of baby bird it was, Peepee took it upon himself to stuff objects into its mouth. My job was to make sure the objects he was stuffing down the baby's throat were edible!

After feeding the baby he would give it a vigorous preening from beak to toe. I would watch on in wonder. I never imagined that the bird I rescued and reared would now be helping me do the very same thing for another bird in need.

By Tracy Pitout, Auckland,
New Zealand

Write to me ... ✉
Email Tracy
kpitout@gmail.com

Our 'flat' cat

My ex-husband and I had been working day in, day out with the owner of a commercial fishing boat, getting the boat ready to take to sea for the fishing season.

It was my birthday, and we had also just got our motorbike on the road after buying it at an auction in boxes of parts. We were excited to finally have it going, and decided to ride it to our favourite bistro for a celebratory dinner.

We were driving along behind a four-wheel drive when the driver suddenly swerved into the next lane. We looked down and saw that he had deliberately moved across to run over a small bundle of fluff. As soon as we could, we did a U-turn and came back to pick up the

111

little bundle. It was a tiny kitten who could just fit into the palm of my hand. His head looked fine, but the rest of his body looked flat!

We took the little kitten home and carefully monitored his progress. His body was young and green and, with plenty of sleep and food, soon healed itself. In just a bit over a week he was acting almost like a normal kitten – eating, sleeping, playing, purring, etc – although his back section was still a bit floppy when he ran. We called him Kitt Kitt.

I think that, because we'd rescued him on the motorbike, Kitt Kitt was quite content to ride on it with us. We would put him in one of the pannier bags on the side, put the lid down and drive off.

He was so obedient that we could take him anywhere. When we arrived at our destination, we'd lift the lid and put him into one of our helmets and tell him to 'Stay!' – just as you would a dog – and carry him around in the helmet. We'd take him to our favourite bistro, put him in one of our helmets, sit the helmet on a chair next to us, tell him to 'Stay!' and he'd stay there all night. Other times, we'd be walking in a shopping centre with him in one of our helmets and he'd be looking out at everything over the rim, just like a little well-trained dog.

The only times he was disobedient were when he could tell we were getting near the local fish shop. Then he'd jump out of the helmet and run straight through to the back of the shop.

Tragedy struck when the boat we were running broke down again. We had to be towed to the nearest Aboriginal settlement to see if we could get parts flown in, and poor Kitt Kitt lost his life on the very rough journey back to port.

I've had other pets since then, but I will always remember Kitt Kitt fondly for his uniqueness. I can still picture his sweet little face and his slightly wobbly walk.

By Elsa Mundy, Atherton Tablelands, North Queensland, Australia

A very special summer

Winki the waxeye arrived at Native Bird Rescue, Wellington after being found on the ground unable to fly. Winki was a young bird with no apparent injuries, so he was put in a cardboard cage with perches, some leafy branches and plenty of room to stretch.

He would take food from a small plastic fork and he amazed me with his enormous appetite. He was also very friendly and tame – so much so that, as he recovered his strength, he spent more and more time out of his cage and in the garden, foraging for his food. He collected insects, nibbled berries and helped himself to the food put out for other birds that were being cared for at the time.

Winki was my constant companion while I tended other injured birds or worked in the garden. He insisted on sleeping in his cardboard cage every night and would fly downstairs each morning for breakfast before he decided what to do for the day. I would stand at the open door with Winki on my shoulder and ask, 'Do you want to practise being a waxeye today, or play "humans"?' Then he would either fly off into the garden or, if the weather was not to his liking, sit on my shoulder while I did the housework or worked in my office.

Visits to the neighbours were a regular event in his social calendar. One highlight was gatecrashing an early Sunday evening barbeque next door where, to my concern, I found him sipping wine as he perched on the rim of a wine glass. I collected a very sleepy little bird that evening.

To the call of 'Winki, Winki, Winki' he would answer with *Twee! Twee!* and come flying from a tree to land on my shoulder. The next five minutes would be an animated series of *twees* and squeaks, telling me everything he had been up to since I last called him, while he snuggled up to my face. He liked bits of banana and a sip of lemon cordial when I stopped for a rest from gardening. Visitors

113

were greeted with enthusiastic *twees* while he sat on their shoulder or head.

This continued over the summer and well into autumn. One stormy night Winki did not want to come in. I watched him fly across the front patio, past the trees and over the road. Two agonising days later he was back, minus most of his tail feathers. He was still able to fly well and he continued visiting me frequently. Then he disappeared again. I called and called, hoping he would return.

Three weeks later I heard his call while I was working in my office. I rushed to the door leading onto the deck next to the kowhai tree and there he was, *twee-ing* excitedly. He hopped down the branch towards me, sat on my finger, then hesitated and jumped off.

I went downstairs to the kitchen to grab a pot of honey and a toothpick. As I scooped a tiny drop of honey onto the toothpick, Winki came down again and licked it. Then he looked up at the branch and hopped back onto it. There was another little waxeye making its way down the branch, calling him. He moved towards his friend and they snuggled up together, *twee-ing* to each other.

The penny dropped … Winki had found a little mate and had brought her 'home' to introduce her to me. The two of them got to work, looking for insects along the branches of the kowhai tree and calling to each other. Winki came down again for some more honey, but quickly went back to his companion and they soon flew off.

I did not see Winki and his mate again, though I often heard him answer me when I called. That was a very special summer – with a very special little bird.

By Karin Wiley, Wellington,
New Zealand

Write to me … ✉

Email Karin
nativebirdrescue@actrix.co.nz

8

Rescued animals are amazing

A feline angel

Valentino is a blind cat who was found on the side of the road and taken to Galway SPCA. We placed him in a home in Galway city with a woman who also had another cat. Unfortunately, after a few weeks she had to give him back because her other cat was terrified of him. Being blind, Valentino kept walking right up to the other cat, which frightened it.

We found another home for him across the city, and he seemed to settle in wonderfully. Then, around eight weeks later, a call came in to our office – Valentino was missing. Four days after that, we got a call from a hotel located a few hundred yards from Valentino's first home, telling us that they had a blind cat outside their door. Yes, it was Valentino!

For Valentino to get to the hotel he had to cross a dual carriageway, go over a bridge, walk through the busiest part of our city where traffic is bumper to bumper, and negotiate at least five roundabouts – not bad for a blind cat.

We decided that, for safety reasons, a new home was the best option for him, so for a while he stayed with us at the SPCA and he ran our city office. The most wonderful thing was that when people met him they did not realise he was blind, he looked so relaxed and at home.

Then one day a girl called Mary walked in, looking to see if we had a blind cat she could adopt. Valentino was on duty that day and he walked up to her and jumped on her knee.

Mary then realised she had met her Valentino. Today, they live happily together. They moved to Mayo and are planning a move to Cork this summer.

Valentino is our wonder cat – truly amazing. I believe he was an angel sent to us to show us our work is not in vain.

By Margaret O'Sullivan,
Galway SPCA, Galway, Ireland

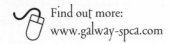 Find out more:
www.galway-spca.com

Write to me …

Email Margaret
osullivan091@eircom.net

Mattie the TV star

Mattie the rabbit arrived at the animal shelter where I volunteer, with her black and white angora fur badly matted and a broken back leg. The kind people at Bunnies Urgently Needing Shelter (BUNS) took Mattie to a vet specialising in rabbit care. He bandaged her leg, shaved off her matted fur and recommended that she not exercise for several weeks so that her broken leg could heal.

Once Mattie's leg was better, her caretaker, Jean, put her out in a 36-inch-high pen to get some exercise. Jean came home that evening to find the pen empty. Mattie had hopped into another rabbit's pen and been bitten. Jean tried to keep Mattie from escaping, but as she could jump 36 inches vertically it was proving to be difficult.

Jean called me up and said she had the perfect rabbit for me. Not only was Mattie a long-haired angora rabbit (my favourite breed), but she could jump really high. I was intrigued. I had been training

Photo provided by Andrea Bratt Frick

Talented Mattie mid-jump

some of my rabbits to jump hurdles and manoeuvre through a rabbit-sized agility course. It would be nice to train such a naturally high leaper, and I had always wanted a black and white angora.

A pair of my trained rabbits had a large enough living area to accommodate a third rabbit. I asked Jean if I could bring my pair, Filbert and Muffy, to meet Mattie at the shelter. BUNS supervises 'dates' for desexed rabbits who are looking for a companion. Filbert, Muffy and Mattie got along well on their date at the BUNS shelter, so I adopted Mattie and brought them all home together.

My new trio of rabbits snuggled, played and trained together. Mattie was a natural at jumping hurdles and soon became the star of the hopping team.

We received an invitation to audition a rabbit for a television show on Animal Planet called *Pet Star*. With help from Mattie's former fosterer, Jean, I began seriously training the rabbits. We used

117

a method called clicker training, which the rabbits really enjoyed. If the bunnies jumped a hurdle, we would make a clicking noise while they were in mid-air and give them a treat or other reward when they landed. Mattie enjoyed jumping hurdles but she really liked to be with her new bunny friends, so her favourite reward became returning to Filbert and Muffy.

Mattie appeared on *Pet Star* in 2003 and competed against several dogs, a pig and some birds. She was very brave for a rabbit, and jumped her hurdle course in front of a live audience, then hopped back to snuggle with Filbert and Muffy.

In January of 2005, a film crew from Japan visited Mattie and filmed her for a television special on amazing animals from all over the world. Mattie jumped over 80 obstacles during the filming!

Mattie and her friends continue to perform at schools, parties, retirement homes, festivals and Easter egg hunts. She has become an ambassador for shelter rabbits, and helps to educate people about rabbit care and behaviour. Mattie has certainly come a long way from being an unwanted rabbit with a broken leg and matted fur that someone dumped at a shelter.

By Andrea Bratt Frick, Carpinteria,
California, United States of America

Write to me ... ✉
Email Andrea
fuzzfarm1@cox.net

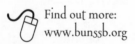 Find out more:
www.bunssb.org

Lost and found

I first saw Ngaro when I was teaching in a south Auckland school. He looked a bit like a spaniel, with soft wavy black hair and a long-haired tail, and had come to school with a boy called Victor.

One day I found Victor in tears. The caretaker was telling him that if the dog came to school again he would have to put him in the swimming pool compound. Once they were in there, dogs were collected by the ranger and taken to the pound, and with so many stray dogs in the area their fate would almost certainly be sealed.

Victor's mother had told him not to bring the dog back home, so I decided to take him but I couldn't leave him by himself all day. The caretaker and I came to an agreement. The dog would sleep in the caretaker's little shed, and I'd come and see him or take him for a walk at lunchtime.

The children, who were nearly all Maori or Pacific Islanders, got very fond of him. They named him Ngaro and told me it was Maori for 'lost'. It seemed appropriate, and so Ngaro he was.

I soon noticed he was bumping into things. If he was excited, he'd run straight into a bicycle tyre or the post of the washing line. When he came to a bank he sometimes just fell rather than jumped down. I took him to the vet and discovered that he was blind.

He still had an instinct to retrieve, loved the water and loved to go after a ball. I trained him to sit in front of me and wait for the command to go. I'd throw the ball over his head, then he would search around for it, going by scent and the sound of the bounce. In the sea he would hear the splash. If he got off course, I threw stones near the ball to point him in the right direction.

When Blind Week came along, I used Ngaro at school to demonstrate what it was like to be blind and how he used his other senses. The children also learned what is involved in caring for an animal, and how our animal companions need love and affection, exercise, water and shelter.

I had Ngaro for a long time. He depended on me, but likewise I would have been 'lost' without him. I had a little 50 cc motorbike and I fixed a box on the back so that he could go everywhere with

119

me. He loved it, his ears flapping in the wind. I'd had him for about 14 years, when one day we rode to the local village where I was now living. I pulled up at the shop and was horrified to see the box was empty. I went back and forth all day and couldn't understand why I couldn't find him. I made photocopies of his photograph and distributed them. I told the police, taxi drivers and bus drivers.

That night there was a big moon in a clear sky as I continued my search, walking and calling, my heart sinking. He was old now and could have tipped out as I zoomed round a corner. Maybe he was lying injured somewhere. Finally I went to bed. Friends came round in the morning to commiserate with me.

Then came a knock at the door. And there was Ngaro with my friend Joy and her daughter Isa. They lived at the bottom of a bush-covered valley on the route I took to the village. They'd opened their door that morning to find Ngaro on the doorstep. Maybe he was stunned by his fall and had hidden all day and night. I'd once taken him to that house, and somehow he'd found his way to it. Not such a remarkable thing for most dogs to do, but I was pleased and proud that my little blind Ngaro had used those other senses to get 'found'. In fact I looked up the Maori word for 'found' but it didn't appeal, so Ngaro he remained for 16 wonderful years of companionship.

By Marion Bridge, Waiheke Island, New Zealand

Write to me …
Email Marion
mabridge@ihug.co.nz

Tim's journey

Tim was a Labrador retriever cross, rescued as a stray on the outskirts of Durham city by a friend of ours. He was in a sorry state, with body sores, visible ribs and a tail like a length of twine. Our friend paid

£67 in vet fees to restore him to a better condition. Unfortunately, Tim and our friend's dog could not get along. Knowing that we had recently lost our well-loved dog aged 15 and a half years, she suggested we might be interested in giving Tim a home. We were, so he came to live with us.

Tim soon settled in and acquired a beautiful coat, a magnificent tail and 'feathery' legs. People were always coming up to say, 'What a lovely dog!' Yes, Tim was indeed lovely, but even lovelier than his appearance was his nature. In the five and a half years we had him, we never heard him growl.

One day during a shopping trip, my husband Ken took Tim down the lane to a patch of ground where Tim could enjoy a romp, while I ran some errands. Afterwards, as arranged, I went to meet them, but coming up the lane was only Ken – no Tim! I was shocked.

Ken explained that Tim had been happily exploring in the grass, when two large dogs had suddenly come up to him with fighting in mind. Tim ran off in a panic into the maze of narrow lanes in the nearby allotments. Ken had been looking and calling for him to no avail. Together, we explored the many lanes of the allotment gardens, asking everyone we met if they had seen Tim. We searched and called for almost two hours but had no luck. I began to dread what might have happened if he had reached the busy main road nearby. Two boys said they had seen a dog matching Tim's description right at the far end of the gardens.

As it was the school holidays, our granddaughter and her friend had called in earlier that day to see us. They had gone up to the town centre, arranging to return for dinner. I realised that it was time we were home to prepare for their arrival, so we set off homeward, feeling sad but determined to resume our search after dinner until it became too dark.

As we walked up from our back gate towards our conservatory, a wonderful sight awaited us. The girls were sitting in the conservatory, and beside them – looking very cool, calm and collected – sat Tim! How thankful we were to see him safe and well.

The girls had seen no sign of him on their way back from town; they had found him sitting at the conservatory door when they arrived. This meant that Tim had found his own way home, a journey over a mile and half long, following a route he'd never been on before, with seven avenues of busy traffic to cross – not to mention two main roads.

Sadly, Tim died of kidney failure after a short illness. The vet said he would have been about ten years old, but we felt that he should have lived longer. Being in our eighties now, we cannot in all fairness have another dog and our lives are definitely the poorer for it.

By Vera Sykes, Ashington,
Northumberland, England

Write to me ... ✉
Mrs Vera Sykes
230 Newbiggin Road
Ashington
Northumberland
NE63 0TW
United Kingdom

A bovine escape artist

For seven long months, after escaping from an auction house in Vermont in April 2005, Annie Dodge the cow wandered the countryside, evading capture and doing her best to survive on her own. Her first month of freedom was difficult, and she wandered far and wide in search of food. Luckily, after trekking across a river and several roads, she found her way into the yard of Barbara and Bill Chamberlain, two long-time members of Farm Sanctuary.

Concerned for Annie's well-being, the Chamberlains graciously welcomed her onto their property and did their best to make her feel at home. Perceiving their kindness, Annie started coming to the Chamberlains' home every night, where she was offered food, shelter and a sense of belonging.

Annie's new foster parents never saw her during the day and they had no idea where she trotted off to after eating dinner in their yard each evening, but they always expected that she would be back the next night and hoped they were helping to make her life a little bit easier. Watching her kick up her heels and frolic as she disappeared back into the woods each night, they felt confident that their kindness was making a difference.

Eventually, the Chamberlains decided to call the local auction house where Annie Dodge had made her escape, but stockyard employees could find no record of the young cow. They offered to slaughter Annie for the Chamberlains, but this was not to be her fate. The kind couple wanted Annie to live out the rest of her life in peace at Farm Sanctuary.

Working with our New York shelter staff, the Chamberlains continued to provide Annie with food and helped her to become more comfortable around people. Because Annie had been wandering alone for so long, this was no easy task. But finally, on October 25, she willingly walked into the Chamberlains' barn on her own, and later that night made the journey to Farm Sanctuary.

Now safe at our New York shelter, Annie Dodge no longer has to be alone. Aptly named in honour of Annie Dodge Wauneka, the first Native American to receive the Presidential Medal of Freedom, she freed herself and now has a lifetime of good health, kind attention and loving companionship to look forward to. Watching Annie Dodge settle into her new home, we can't help but be impressed by her courage and fierce independence. Now living alongside many other daring souls – including cows Cinci Freedom and Queenie, who both escaped from slaughterhouses – she is in good company.

From Farm Sanctuary,
Watkins Glen, New York,
United States of America

Find out more:
www.farmsanctuary.org

Write to us ... ✉

Farm Sanctuary
3150 Aikens Road
Watkins Glen, NY 14891
USA
email: info@farmsanctuary.org

Educating Dewdrop

Dewdrop was the smallest of three kittens but she made the biggest impression. Just a bit of grey fluff with satellite-dish eyes, she was already a problem child. At three weeks of age, Dewdrop and her two sisters were orphaned when their mother was hit by a car. The shelter that picked them up had to move them along. They had been exposed to an infection, and required close monitoring and possibly treatment.

'Be prepared,' the director warned me. 'Rhinotracheitis can kill kittens.' My allergies made a long-term relationship unrealistic, so my plan was to nurse the kittens back to health until the shelter's next adoption day.

The snag in my plan reared its ugly head with a sneeze. One minute Dewdrop was sitting up sniffling, the next she was lying across her saucer panting. I rushed her to the vet, who discovered that not only did she have an infection, she also had a heart murmur and a potassium deficiency. She had neurological damage as well, which explained her wobbly walk. According to the vet, her mother had been incubating a virus that had damaged Dewdrop.

Perhaps it's the special-education teacher in me, but I worried that no one else could love and understand her. I sent her sisters off to adoption day but couldn't part with Dewdrop. Equipped with an air filter to mediate our relationship, I set about educating my special-needs baby.

She would miss some of her jumps, trip over her tail and fall off the bed in the middle of the night. I called her name so many times to warn her of impending danger that she became Didi for expediency. My clumsy cat would need lots of support and stimulation to close the gap with her peers, and I was determined to scout out the right resources.

I shopped the way any mom of a potential high achiever does – for vitamins, supplements and educational toys, not for silly pompoms or rattles. Puzzles were good. I settled on a ladybug encased in a wire ball, a bird that popped out of a hollow tree and a remote control mouse. I even hid toys in boots and under blankets to stimulate problem-solving skills.

Didi studied the ball for a few seconds, then yanked the bug out and trotted away carrying it in her teeth, tail held high. She smacked the bird so hard it flew off its spring, and she looked very disappointed when I couldn't figure out how to fix it. The mouse held her interest for a while, until she realised that she could outrun it. In the end, I was the one whose problem-solving skills were being challenged.

Not only did she dig toys out of shoes, she even flipped open the lid of her toy box and helped herself to a bag of catnip. I came home to find the narcotic strewn across the floor and my baby lying belly up, her eyes glazed. She waved one limp paw at me in vague recognition.

Penetrating the forbidden became an engrossing occupation for Didi. It wasn't long before she learned to hook her paw under

125

cupboard doors and pull outward to let herself in. Whenever I stayed out later than she was accustomed to, I would come home to an apartment that looked like it had been burgled. Shopping bags, laundry and stationery would be scattered everywhere, but Didi was always perched on the sofa, her silver paws tucked primly under her chest, her face radiating serenity.

I tried installing hooks on the cupboard doors, but she just flicked them open and sauntered away. The point, after all, was not that she needed anything from the cupboard. It was simply to psyche me out.

Maybe it was the strain of trying to keep up with her that made me take up yoga. In any case, I discovered that she is as compassionate as she is clever. The first time I stretched out on the floor to take deep cleansing breaths, she charged at me lopsidedly and stood over my body, swaying, looking intently at my mouth. She probably thought I was the one with a heart condition.

Didi reads people like a map, zeroing in on a direct route to their hearts. She avoids tense, angry people but has infinite patience for seniors and tail-grabbing babies. Her ability to feel when people need company is uncanny.

There is a lady who sits in our community garden with her head dropped in her hands like a lily on a broken stem. She never looks up at anyone who talks to her, except her grandchildren, who come to the park to take her home. Didi, however, is on a mission and will not be deterred. Wearing her little harness, with me following discreetly behind, she pads over tipsily and raises her pond-green eyes to the woman's hands. Only then does the lady look up and brighten. I feel like the clumsy one and Didi becomes the picture of quiet grace. Perhaps Didi's faltering steps have touched the woman, showing her that even a damaged vessel can draw pleasure from life.

Photo provided by Linda Handiak

Dewdrop: a small cat with a big heart

The vets said that Didi would never be big and that her heart would always be weak. They were wrong. Her heart is big and strong enough to absorb someone else's pain.

Footnote: I would like to thank the Animal Rescue Network of Montreal for being so supportive during Didi's health crises.

By Linda Handiak, Montreal, Quebec, Canada

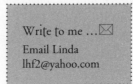

Write to me ... ✉

Email Linda
lhf2@yahoo.com

Will it rain today?

One day in Melbourne many years ago, my husband's grandmother was busily working in her front garden. A car pulled to a sudden stop in front of her house and then sped off. She looked up from her gardening and saw that left behind in the middle of the road was a tiny black and white kitten of only a few weeks old.

The little kitten seemed to recognise immediately that he had found someone who would save him. Nana told us later that he screamed to her with all the strength his little body could muster and ran on his little legs as fast as he could towards her. She took him inside her house and gave him some water and food. Although he was very thin, he was a very pretty little kitten. He had black fur and snow-white markings, which were a bib and four little socks.

However, Nana had already rescued a gorgeous cat who presided at her house, and my husband's parents (who lived next door to her) were already owned by another two rescued cats. So they named him Timothy and brought him over to our new house in a basket – and he won our hearts and moved in with us immediately. He grew into a loving and playful cat who enjoyed life and living with us. He also grew into a very handsome cat, and spent a great deal of time grooming.

As time went on, however, we realised that Timothy had quite an extraordinary talent. He was an exceptionally good rain forecaster. We noticed that, while he carefully washed his beautiful coat all over every day, he only ever washed his ears just before rain. In fact, he would wash his ears exactly two days before rain. Even more amazing was the fact that the harder he washed his ears the harder it rained. As he always washed very carefully after each meal, spending a great deal of time to look his beautiful best, it was easy for us to be able to see him washing – and be the first in Melbourne to accurately know when rain was expected and whether it would be light showers or a downpour!

Our family knew to take raincoats and umbrellas with them on Timothy's predicted rain days, even when it didn't look as if it was going to rain, and we used his talent when deciding on weekend activities, washing the car and watering the garden.

None of our other cats have had this talent, and we certainly missed Timothy's forecasts when he died of cancer at nine and a half years of age. We would never have guessed, when we took in this abandoned little kitten, that he would turn out to be our very own accurate Bureau of Meteorology!

By Suzanne Coomes, Canterbury, Victoria, Australia

The clever little Westie

While working in animal welfare in Cape Town, South Africa, I was often called out to rescue strays. One Saturday afternoon I was called to collect a stray dog seen running around the harbour area of Hout Bay. I managed, after some coaxing, to collect a nervous but delightful little male West Highland terrier.

As it was late afternoon the kennels were closed, and I wasn't going there until the next morning. I couldn't keep the dog at our house as I already had two dogs and eight cats of my own. I took him home, however, while I called the local vet. I drove from the harbour to our house, which was in a security complex controlled by an electronic gate and surrounded by electric fencing. I carried the little Westie in through our front door, through the lounge area and out to our walled garden. Then I telephoned the local vet and asked him if he could hold the Westie overnight and I would collect him in the morning on my way to the kennels. He agreed, and I carried the little dog out to the car and drove him to the vet's.

When I arrived home, some ten minutes later, I received a call from the receptionist at the vet's to say the Westie had escaped. The vet's was at least five miles away from the harbour so we weren't sure if he would head back there or not, or what would happen if he did as there were a few busy roads to cross.

I was hoping he might know where he lived and head back there. I then looked into my garden and saw, much to my surprise, the little Westie. Somehow, after he'd escaped from the vet's, he had made it back to my house. But how did he know where to go? He'd been driven to my house from the harbour, and then driven in the opposite direction from my house to the vet's. He'd been carried through my front door to the walled back garden, which was indistinguishable from those of my neighbours, yet he knew which one was mine – as well as entering a security complex which had electronically controlled gates!

The next day he was taken to our kennels and, as he wasn't claimed within seven days, he was adopted by one of our volunteers and now lives a life of spoilt luxury.

I would still like to know how he found my house from the vet's. After all, I had only collected him from the harbour area that afternoon and he'd only been at my house for the length of time it took me to make a phone call to the vet's – about five minutes in total. Rescued animals truly are 'smarter than Jack'.

By Steve Maxworthy,
Greek Animal Welfare Fund,
London, England

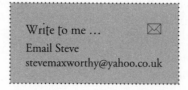

Write to me …

Email Steve
stevemaxworthy@yahoo.co.uk

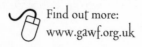

Find out more:
www.gawf.org.uk

9

Smart people rescue animals

SPCA to the rescue

Back in the early 1980s my husband and I decided to get a Burmese cat, Cosmo, to complement our ageing sealpoint Siamese cat, Marcus. Cosmo fitted into our lifestyle but only on his terms. I'd never known a cat who was so arrogant. However, we got along just fine until one day, several months after he'd come to live with us, he didn't come home as usual.

In the early hours of the morning I could hear a constant meowing that seemed to be coming from the next street, and went to investigate. There was Cosmo on the apex of the roof of a neighbour's two-storey house, howling his head off – at 3 am. I reluctantly called out to him, worried I would wake the neighbours, but it only made Cosmo howl more. So I decided to leave him in his predicament until daybreak, hoping that he would have come down by then.

By mid-morning the next day he was still there, despite several attempts to cajole him down. So off I went to talk to the owner of the house, to see if I could get on the roof and talk Cosmo down. But the owner of the house would not allow me on the roof. I could see that Cosmo was uncomfortable as his feet appeared to be causing him pain. He wanted to come down but was petrified. It was a very steep roof and he was only balancing on the top of a curved tile.

In desperation I rang the police for advice – no luck there. By this time it was late afternoon. I rang the fire department; they told me that Cosmo would come down when he was hungry. I asked the house owner again, but no luck there either. Poor Cosmo was noticeably in pain and quite stressed at this point. Neighbours were collecting around the house calling out to him, which added to his anxiety.

Then I had a brainwave; I don't know why I hadn't thought of it earlier. I rang the SPCA and explained Cosmo's plight. Their response was, 'We're on our way, see you soon!' and they were there in no time at all.

The SPCA inspector rescued Cosmo with a special extension ladder and there were shouts of glee from the bystanders. The inspector had a few choice words to say to the house owner.

Poor Cosmo's paws were cut and bleeding and all I wanted to do was get him home, treat his wounds and feed him. Eventually I managed to slip him away from my neighbours and get him back home.

But Cosmo's adventure was not quite over yet. He refused his food and took off into the backyard, where I observed him limping around the garden, sniffing at everything. When he was satisfied that everything was okay in his territory, he finally came inside, ate his meal and instantly entered the land of Nod, draped over his food bowl. I'm sure he had a smile on his face – I know I did.

By June Spragg, Warkworth,
New Zealand

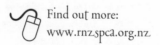 Find out more:
www.rnz.spca.org.nz

Write to me …
Email June
junespragg@ihug.co.nz

Juniper gets a new leg

Juniper was taken in by a woman who was at a farm attempting to press charges against the farmer for neglect of his dog. She witnessed a tiny goat hopping across the filthy yard, bent nearly in half and actually walking on her front legs. The goat, later named Juniper, had only three quarters of her back left leg and no hoof on her back right leg. Sharp bone protruded through both back legs, and she was dehydrated and malnourished.

The tips of both her ears were missing and her body was covered with lice. With threats to turn the man in for yet another incident of neglect, the farmer told the woman that he had purchased the goat at auction in that condition but that the woman could take her. Juniper was brought to an SPCA, cleaned up and treated by a local vet. Once her legs had healed, the woman contacted Farm Sanctuary.

Juniper arrived at our New York shelter and, seeing the condition she was in, we made immediate plans to take her to Cornell University's animal orthopaedic department. The doctors speculated that the cause of the damage to her ears and legs was untreated frostbite, and that the frostbite had resulted in sharp bone which had actually worked through the skin of the two back legs.

To prevent the bone from protruding any further, the back left leg would have to be removed or Juniper would attempt to use it, damaging the area further. However, once the left leg was removed, all of her weight would shift to her back right leg with no hoof, causing further damage. We consulted with a horse prosthetist, Mr Frank, who felt that he could design a suitable limb for Juniper.

After weeks of discussion, the decision to have Juniper receive a prosthesis was made. Juniper then underwent surgery to partially amputate the sharp bone but retaining the joint for easier movement of the leg. This surgery went well and the area healed quickly over

133

the next few weeks. A cast was taken to fit her for the prosthesis. Mr Frank then created her new leg, which she took to instantly. After just two fittings, Juniper was off and running.

Progressing from the frustration of barely being able to get around to frolicking and playing in the grass has done wonders for Juniper's state of mind. She is happy and confident, and no longer shies away when people visit. Even when she is not wearing her prosthetic leg – and sometimes she prefers not to – she is active and joyful. Because Juniper requires constant monitoring by her prosthetist, she will remain here at Farm Sanctuary and will not be adopted out to another home.

From Farm Sanctuary,
Watkins Glen, New York,
United States of America

Find out more:
www.farmsanctuary.org

Write to us … ✉

Farm Sanctuary
3150 Aikens Road
Watkins Glen, NY 14891
USA
email: info@farmsanctuary.org

The animals' young friend

Ansh Mehta from Mumbai, India is only four years old, but he already shows a great sense of compassion for animals.

One morning, Ansh was out riding his bicycle with some of his friends when he suddenly noticed a group of crows pecking an owl. The little bird was obviously in need of help. Ansh scared the crows away, and stood guarding the owl until they flew away in disgust.

Ansh then called his neighbour, Swati Shah, who works at PETA India. With Swati's help, Ansh picked up Raja – as he had named the owl – with a towel, and took him to the nearest vet to look him over. The vet discovered that, thanks to Ansh's timely intervention, the

Photo provided by PETA India

Lucky Raja the owl

crows had fortunately managed to inflict very little damage on Raja. He advised Ansh to keep Raja in a large basket in a dark room until the evening. Because owls sleep during the day, Raja would have been disoriented by the daylight. Later that night, Ansh released Raja back into the wild where he belongs.

Whenever Ansh sees an animal in distress, he stops to help it. Since he is so young, he makes sure that a knowledgeable person who can handle animals is there with him. The one thing he never does is walk away from an animal in trouble. Compassionate children lead to compassionate adults.

From PETA India, Mumbai, India

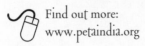 Find out more:
www.petaindia.org

Write to us ... ✉
PETA India
People for the Ethical
Treatment of Animals
PO Box 28260
Juhu, Mumbai – 400 049
India
email: info@petaindia.org

135

Junkyard pony

When I was 14 years old, my papa and I would walk our dog every night through the quiet streets of our country town. We usually took time to detour past the paddock with the hairy brown horse in it, our pockets packed with carrots for this lonely boy.

The paddock was next to a car wrecker's yard, and skeletons of cars had spilled over the fence and lay rusting and sinking into the ground. The ancient barbed wire fences were drooping all over the place, and I often wondered why the beautiful brown horse didn't simply step through and run away from this junkyard to greener pastures.

Despite his squalid home, the brown horse was always happy to see us, letting me step through the wires to scratch the base of his neck, run my hands over his fat belly and whisper pretty words into his furry ears.

One night, having not walked past his paddock for a few days, Dad and I came upon the brown horse lying on his side and struggling to get up. We climbed through the sagging fence and tried to coax him up, but it soon became obvious that this wouldn't work.

Dad got on his cellphone and called the SPCA, while I ran home for a bucket of water. The SPCA already knew about the horse and his owners, and within an hour the owners were in the paddock trying to get the big boy up. The problem was, he'd been left for so long and become so fat that he'd finally foundered. On top of this, his hooves had been left untended for so long that they had splayed to the size of dinner plates and split most of the way up.

Dad and I watched in horror as, having finally got the brown horse onto his feet, the owners proceeded to hack away at his hooves with common house tools. The poor boy was left standing miserably on his now square-shaped hooves.

The owners realised that the big horse needed a lot of TLC to get him healthy again, and decided that it would be better to send him to the meatworks. However, my dad wasn't having any of that and, instead, paid them there and then the amount they would have received from the meatworks.

So the big brown boy came to live with my family, my horse and my little sister's pony. I walked him everywhere all summer and worked with his feet every day – even though he hated people touching them. By the end of summer I had a beautiful big brown horse, almost the right weight, and hooves that were starting to look horse-like again.

The brown horse came into his own and was an absolute joy to be around – so much fun, and so eager to please! Eventually he moved on to a new home – one with many children to love him, as my family had done. Yay for the junkyard pony!

By Emmylou Cooke, Featherston, New Zealand

Matt the Afghan cat's amazing adventure

Matt was rescued by US military soldiers in Afghanistan. During the long journey to the home of his new owner, Greg McDermott, in Georgia, USA, the flight stopped in Gander, Newfoundland. The soldiers decided to tie a belt around Matt and take him out for a few minutes for some fresh air. The noise from the plane spooked Matt and he ran off.

Canadian Customs notified us at Gander and Area SPCA of the situation. That evening I went up to the airport and walked round the area where he was last seen. There was no sign of him. Two days later we were told that he had been spotted. I searched the area again for about 40 minutes. Then, when I looked down, there he was

137

hiding in an old tree stump, not one foot away from me. But when I reached for him he took off, with the belt dragging behind him.

Over the next two evenings there was no sign of him. I even called his owner Greg for advice. Before I had the chance to go up to the airport again, I received a call from a dog walker who had spotted Matt in the same area. Just as I was going down the road I saw a gentleman standing with Matt in his arms, who said he had found him lying in the woods.

Matt was brought to the shelter. The belt was clearly causing him great discomfort, so I cut it off. He gave a sigh and lay down on the blanket. He had no interest in food – he was just too exhausted.

Happily, Matt recovered from his ordeal and was united with Greg in Georgia.

By Bonnie Harris,
Gander and Area SPCA,
Newfoundland, Canada

 Find out more:
www.envision.ca/webs/
ganderandareaspca

Write to us …   ✉

Gander and Area SPCA
36 McCurdy Drive
Gander, NL A1V 1A2
Canada
email: ganderspca@hotmail.com

A little boy with a big heart

photo
p84

Eight-year-old Zubin Bhatt lives in Baroda, India. He comes from a family of animal protectors and spends his day tending to the abandoned animals who have made his house their home.

Zubin's home and heart are open to all animals and, among others, he takes care of a donkey, many kittens, some eagles and a calf.

One day, Zubin heard a ruckus outside his window and was shocked to see people trying to kill a snake who had found his way into the building. He raced down and spoke to the people, then helped them to capture the snake humanely. Knowing that snakes are a protected species, Zubin helped rehabilitate the reptile and return him to his real home – the jungle.

From PETA India, Mumbai, India

Find out more:
www.petaindia.org

Write to us ... ✉

PETA India
People for the Ethical
Treatment of Animals
PO Box 28260
Juhu, Mumbai – 400 049
India
email: info@petaindia.org

My, BettyJo, what few teeth you have!

A cattle dog named BettyJo was rescued from New Orleans after Hurricane Katrina. She travelled all the way from New Orleans to Canada, where she was put up for adoption at the Cambridge and District Humane Society.

The shelter staff made a gruesome discovery when they looked into BettyJo's mouth: her teeth were worn down so much that the nerve endings were exposed. Ouch! Despite her obvious dental pain, she was a sweet and lovable dog.

So the shelter booked BettyJo an appointment with a nearby dental and oral veterinary surgeon. The vet determined that BettyJo had had mange prior to her rescue and it had made her so itchy that she had chewed at herself excessively, causing her gums to recede and abrasive wear to her teeth.

The Cambridge and District Humane Society held a fund-raiser for the 'BettyJo Fund' to help pay for the expensive dental surgery. Her surgery was successful; however, she had to have

139

14 teeth removed. Due to her lack of teeth, BettyJo can now eat only moistened dog food.

The shelter found the perfect home for BettyJo with me and my two cats, Buddy and Purrcy. She quickly adjusted to the cold Canadian weather and actually loves playing in the snow. Luckily for BettyJo, she doesn't need her teeth to catch snowflakes!

By Doug Elsey, Cambridge, Ontario, Canada

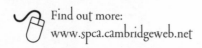 Find out more:
www.spca.cambridgeweb.net

Found in the nick of time

Early one Sunday morning my husband and I drove past an extremely emaciated dog following an elderly man. We could clearly see the dog's ribs though his skin. We drove on to our appointment in tears and promised ourselves that we would go back and look for the dog – we were even willing to pay for him to be put down so that he would not suffer any more.

Three hours later we got back to the area and spent 45 minutes looking for the dog, but could not find him. I prayed that someone really nice would find this dog and take care of him, and we decided to head back home. Just as we turned the corner I saw a speck of orange lying in a field. I screamed that I had found him, and we pulled over and called out to the dog. He raised his head slightly out of the grass and his expression seemed to say, *Are you calling ME?* He could no longer stand so my husband scooped him up.

We went to an emergency animal hospital. The dog weighed only 36 pounds – his ideal weight was 71 pounds. He had bite marks all over his head, he was blind in his right eye, and a bony part of his spine had broken through his skin. When we were told he could be saved, we were hiccuping with tears. I named him Toby.

It took close to a year to get Toby healthy. We bought a special harness that wrapped around his belly to help him walk. His skin integrity was so poor that sores broke out on his tail. As a result, his tail died and we had to have it docked. The vet initially thought Toby had a form of blood cancer because his body was no longer producing red blood cells, but this was found to be due to dehydration. She told my husband she believed that, at the moment when we found Toby, he had actually lain down to die.

Toby has been with us now for four years. He needs to take behavioural medication and he is monitored by Purdue University's animal behavioural clinic. We just love him, and he gives us the greatest amount of joy as well as heartache.

By Deborah Lafata, Plainfield, Indiana, United States of America

Fast food feline

I found Sam on July 9, 2005 when I detoured into a fast food restaurant on the way to the airport. There he was, a tiny kitten who looked to be on the brink of death.

I caught him easily, decided to skip the food, and put him in a basket in my car with cat food and water. He found his way to the back dashboard and slept until we arrived home four hours later.

He had worms and fleas, could hardly walk and at eight weeks old barely weighed one pound. Now he is a healthy and lively cat who fetches better than most dogs. He prefers to fetch sparkly puffs but he also has a Santa hat that he enjoys playing with.

Sam gets along with all of our cats and has been a special friend to Charlie, a tiny kitten I found the following October. He washes

141

Charlie and sleeps with him. All of my rescued cats are very loving and grateful, and we're thankful to have them in our lives.

By Lisa Beyer, Animal Rescue Foundation, Milledgeville, Georgia, United States of America

Find out more:
www.animalrescuefoundation.org

Just like the movies

back cover

This story sounds like a movie plot – but it happened in real life.

I am a college student in Tucson, Arizona. I spent the summer of 2005 in a rancho (which is like a little village) in Mexico with my aunt and uncle. While I was there, I befriended a dog, Jack, whose owners no longer wanted or cared for him. They asked if I would take him but, since I knew I'd be leaving in a few months, I told them I could only take care of him while I was there.

Jack was very skinny and afraid of everything because he had been neglected. Within a week, when he realised I would feed him and wouldn't hurt him, he became very attached to me. He would follow me everywhere. The few times he lost me, he ran frantically round the rancho, searching for me. We were inseparable.

A little boy from his old family told me that Jack was lucky I gave him food, because all he got at his old home were kicks. I was very sad to leave Jack when I went back home, but I knew my aunt would feed him and he would keep her company (my aunt has diabetes and can barely walk due to extensive leg injuries).

In October 2005 my family and I made another trip to Mexico. I found out that Jack now went back and forth between his old home and my aunt's house. I was also told that he had 'accidentally' fallen into a well and was stuck there for three days before my uncle could get him out. What is odd about that is that the well was on the land of an old lady who is known for her hatred of dogs and for poisoning them. While I was there, Jack again followed me round the whole time – he knew I was his real mommy. Although I was worried about him, I had to return to the United States with my family. All I could do was keep Jack in my prayers.

In February 2006 my dad went back to Mexico. Upon his return home, he informed me that Jack had gone back to live at his old home but, since they didn't want him, they had abandoned him in the nearest town, San Felipe. I was so upset that I began searching the internet for information on what type of paperwork needed to be done to bring Jack across the border and home with me, where he'd be safe and loved forever – assuming I could find him.

During my search, I came across the website of Mex-Can Pet Partners. They are a non-profit society based in British Columbia, Canada, whose mission is to raise awareness and funds in order to assist their 'partner group', Amigos de los Animales de Guanajuato in Guanajuato, Mexico, to carry out their animal welfare programmes. What is amazing is that the town where Jack had been abandoned was in Guanajuato!

There are so many neglected and abused animals in Mexico, and – given local attitudes to animals in general – I was amazed to find a Mexican-based organisation whose mission was to help them. What was even more amazing was that this organisation responded to my email and physically went to look for Jack. They put up posters offering a reward, and went to the rancho to talk to my uncle to see if he could help them find Jack. They even gave my aunt money to help with her medical care.

My uncle actually found Jack, and Amigos de los Animales de Guanajuato went and picked him up and cared for him. They gave him his shots, bathed him, neutered him and kept me updated almost daily with any new developments. I knew they would take good care of him until we could be reunited.

After exploring many different options for getting Jack to the United States, we decided to fly him further north in Mexico and I would go and pick him up. The date was set and I couldn't have been more excited. My friend drove me down, but on the way we got run off the road and stuck in the snow. Thankfully, someone stopped to help us and we were only two hours late to pick up Jack from the airport – but they were still the longest two hours of my life.

When Jack saw me he became hysterical, screaming and crying, desperate to get out of his kennel and greet me. It was such a great moment. He knew I was his mom and I was there to take care of him.

If Mex-Can Pet Partners and Amigos de los Animales de Guanajuato hadn't helped me, I may never have found Jack and then who knows what would have become of him. They not only took the time to find him, care for him and prepare all his paperwork for travelling across the border, but they actually flew him right to me and his new home. There are few people who would go through so much trying to help another person, let alone a dog. These people are amazing!

When I met Jack, he was skinny and afraid of everything. Now 'poor Jack' is no longer poor but happy, healthy and, most importantly, part of a family.

By Rocio Fonseca, Tucson, Arizona,
United States of America

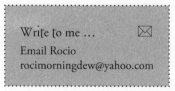

Write to me ...

Email Rocio
rocimorningdew@yahoo.com

The SMARTER than JACK story

We hope you've enjoyed this book. The SMARTER than JACK books are exciting and entertaining to create and so far we've raised over NZ$400,000 to help animals. We are thrilled!

Here's my story about how the SMARTER than JACK series came about.

Until late 1999 my life was a seemingly endless search for the elusive 'fulfilment'. I had this feeling that I was put on this earth to make a difference, but I had no idea how. Coupled with this, I had low self-confidence – not a good combination! This all left me feeling rather frustrated, lonely and unhappy with life. I'd always had a creative streak and loved animals. In my early years I spent many hours designing things such as horse saddles, covers and cat and dog beds. I even did a stint as a professional pet photographer.

Then I remembered something I was once told: do something for the right reasons and good things will come. So that's what I did. I set about starting Avocado Press and creating the first New Zealand edition in the SMARTER than JACK series. It was released in 2002 and all the profit went to the Royal New Zealand SPCA.

Good things did come. People were thrilled to be a part of the book and many were first-time writers. Readers were enthralled and many were delighted to receive the book as a gift from friends and family. The Royal New Zealand SPCA was over $43,000 better off and I received many encouraging letters and emails from readers and contributors. What could be better than that?

How could I stop there! It was as if I had created a living thing with the SMARTER than JACK series; it seemed to have a life all of its own. I now had the responsibility of evolving it. It had to continue to benefit animals and people by providing entertainment, warmth and something that people could feel part of. What an awesome responsibility and opportunity, albeit a bit of a scary one!

It is my vision to make SMARTER than JACK synonymous with smart animals, and a household name all over the world. The concept is already becoming well known as a unique and effective way for animal welfare charities to raise money, to encourage additional donors and to instil a greater respect for animals. The series is now in Australia, New Zealand, the United States of America, Canada and the United Kingdom.

Avocado Press, as you may have guessed, is a little different. We are about more than just creating books; we're about sharing information and experiences, and developing things in innovative ways. Ideas are most welcome too.

We feel it's possible to run a successful business that is both profitable and that contributes to animal welfare in a significant way. We want people to enjoy and talk about our books; that way, ideas are shared and the better it becomes for everyone.

Thank you for reading my story.

Jenny Campbell
Creator of SMARTER than JACK

Submit a story for our books

We are always creating more exciting books in the SMARTER than JACK series. Your true stories are continually being sought.

You can have a look at our website www.smarterthanjack.com. Here you can read stories, find information on how to submit stories, and read entertaining and interesting animal news. You can also sign up to receive the Story of the Week by email. We'd love to hear your ideas, too, on how to make the next books even better.

Guidelines for stories

- The story must be true and about an amazing animal or animals.
- The story should be about 100 to 1000 words in length. We may edit it and you will be sent a copy to approve prior to publication.
- The story must be written from your point of view, not the animal's.
- Photographs and illustrations are welcome if they enhance the story.
- Submissions can be sent by post to SMARTER than JACK (see addresses on the following page) or via the website at www.smarterthanjack.com.
- Include your name, postal and email address, and phone number, and indicate if you do not wish your name to be included with your story.
- Handwritten submissions are perfectly acceptable, but if you can type them, so much the better.
- Posted submissions will not be returned unless a stamped self-addressed envelope is provided.
- The writers of stories selected for publication will be notified prior to publication.
- Stories are welcome from everybody, and given the charitable nature of our projects there will be no prize money awarded, just recognition for successful submissions.

- Particpating animal welfare charities and Avocado Press have the right to publish extracts from the stories received without restriction of location or publication, provided the publication of those extracts helps promote the SMARTER than JACK series.

Where to send your submission

Online

- Use the submission form at www.smarterthanjack.com or email it to submissions@smarterthanjack.com

By post

- **In Australia**
  PO Box 170, Ferntree Gully, VIC 3156, Australia
- **In Canada and the United States of America**
  PO Box 819, Tottenham, ON, L0G 1W0, Canada
- **In New Zealand and rest of world**
  PO Box 27003, Wellington, New Zealand

Don't forget to include your contact details. Note that we may use the information you provide to send you further information about the SMARTER than JACK series. If you do not wish for us to do this, please let us know.

Receive a SMARTER than JACK gift pack

Did you know that around half our customers buy the SMARTER than JACK books as gifts? We appreciate this and would like to thank and reward those who do so. If you buy eight books in the SMARTER than JACK series we will send you a free gift pack.

All you need to do is buy your eight books and either attach the receipt for each book or, if you ordered by mail, just write the date that you placed the order in one of the spaces on the next page. Then complete your details on the form, cut out the page and post it to us. We will then send you your SMARTER than JACK gift pack. Feel free to photocopy this form – that will save cutting a page out of the book.

Do you have a dog or a cat? You can choose from either a cat or dog gift pack. Just indicate your preference.

Note that the contents of the SMARTER than JACK gift pack will vary from country to country, but may include:
- The SMARTER than JACK mini Collector Series
- SMARTER than JACK postcards or bookmarks
- Soft animal toy
- Books in the SMARTER than JACK series

Show your purchases here:

Book 1	Book 2	Book 3	Book 4
Receipt attached ☐ *or* Date ordered _____	Receipt attached ☐ *or* Date ordered _____	Receipt attached ☐ *or* Date ordered _____	Receipt attached ☐ *or* Date ordered _____
Book 5	Book 6	Book 7	Book 8
Receipt attached ☐ *or* Date ordered _____	Receipt attached ☐ *or* Date ordered _____	Receipt attached ☐ *or* Date ordered _____	Receipt attached ☐ *or* Date ordered _____

Complete your details:

Your name: _____

Street address: _____

City/town: _____

State: _____

Postcode: _____

Country: _____

Phone: _____

Email: _____

Would you like a cat or dog gift pack?   CAT/DOG

Post the completed page to us:

- **In Australia**
  PO Box 170, Ferntree Gully, VIC 3156, Australia
- **In Canada and the United States of America**
  PO Box 819, Tottenham, ON, L0G 1W0, Canada
- **In New Zealand and rest of world**
  PO Box 27003, Wellington, New Zealand

Please allow four weeks for delivery.

Which animal charities do we help?

At SMARTER than JACK we work with many charities around the world. Below is a list of some of the charities that benefit from the sale of our books. For a more complete list please visit www.smarterthanjack.com. If would like your charity to benefit from SMARTER than JACK please contact us by email: info@smarterthanjack.com.

New Zealand

Royal New Zealand SPCA and their branches and member societies: www.rnzspca.org.nz

Australia

RSPCA Australia and their eight state and territory member Societies: www.rspca.org.au

United Kingdom

Several animal welfare organisations in the United Kingdom

Canada

The Canadian Federation of Humane Societies and their participating member societies: www.cfhs.ca

United States of America

Around 25 humane societies, welfare leagues and SPCAs from all over the United States of America

Get more wonderful stories

Now you can receive a fantastic new-release SMARTER than JACK book every three months. That's a new book every March, June, September and December. The books are delivered to your door. It's easy!

Every time you get a book you will also receive a copy of our members-only newsletter. Postage is included in the subscription price if the delivery address is in Canada, the United Kingdom, Australia or New Zealand.

You can also purchase existing titles in the SMARTER than JACK series. To purchase a book go to your local bookstore or visit our website **www.smarterthanjack.com** and select the participating charity that you would like to benefit from your purchase.

How your purchase will help animals

The amount our partner animal welfare charities receive varies according to how the books are sold and the country in which they are sold. Contact your local participating animal welfare charity for more information.